Concept-Based Curriculum and Instruction for the Thinking Classroom

H. LYNN ERICKSON

foreword by Carol Ann Tomlinson

CORWIN PRESS
A SAGE Publications Company
Thousand Oaks, California

For information:

Corwin Press
A Sage Publications Company
2455 Teller Road
Thousand Oaks, California 91320
E-mail: order@corwinpress.com

Sage Publications Ltd.
1 Oliver's Yard
55 City Road
London EC1Y 1SP
United Kingdom

Sage Publications India Pvt. Ltd.
B-42, Panchsheel Enclave
Post Box 4109
New Delhi 110 017 India

Printed in the United States of America.

Library of Congress Cataloging-in-Publication Data

Erickson, H. Lynn.
Concept-based curriculum and instruction for the thinking classroom / H. Lynn Erickson.
    p. cm.
Includes bibliographical references and index.
ISBN 978-1-4129-1699-8 (cloth) — ISBN 978-1-4129-1700-1 (pbk.)
   1. Curriculum planning—United States. 2. Education—Curricula—Standards—United States. 3. Interdisciplinary approach in education—United States. I. Title.
LB2806.15.E752 2007
375.001—dc22

                                         2006006257

This book is printed on acid-free paper.

10 11 12 13 14 12 11 10 9 8

Acquisitions Editor:	Faye Zucker
Editorial Assistant:	Gem Rabanera
Project Editor:	Tracy Alpern
Copy Editor:	Brenda Weight
Proofreader:	Andrea Martin
Typesetter:	C&M Digitals (P) Ltd.
Indexer:	Pamela Van Huss
Cover Designer:	Scott Van Atta

Concept-Based
Curriculum
and Instruction
for the
Thinking
Classroom

*Dedicated to teachers and administrators the world over, who are
on the concept-based journey to nurture the minds and hearts of young people.*

Contents

List of Figures
and Charts

Chapter 1

Chapter 2

Foreword

I wish I had been able to learn from Lynn Erickson's work a long time ago.

Like many teachers, I spent a considerable classroom career trying to figure out how to make *what* I taught compelling for the students *whom* I taught. No one in a position of authority told me I needed to do that. Rather, I saw the difference in students when I was able to make curriculum "appealing." I had no formal way of accomplishing that. Again like many teachers, I just "gutted" it out.

My approach to curriculum design went through various iterations as I developed as a teacher. In my earliest years, I suppose my plan of action was to try to learn enough at home on Monday night to have something to tell my students on Tuesday, to learn enough Tuesday night to have something to tell them on Wednesday—and so on, for what inevitably proved to be an exhausting year. I had one instinct that served me well, however. I knew I wanted to make the content interesting to the students. In my earliest days as a teacher, that meant making some connections with their lives and experiences, telling stories, and throwing in an occasional game.

Somewhat later, I worked with colleagues who agreed that we had two key imperatives in curriculum design—to make curriculum "fun," and to be very sure we focused on "what mattered most" for students to learn. We saw evidence daily in both student motivation and achievement that we were onto something useful. Those goals, too, were sensible, it turns out.

My thinking about the goals, however, wasn't as sharply defined as it should have been. I now think of curriculum as being "engaging" instead of "fun." I'm not opposed to students experiencing pleasure in their work; pleasure is a kid magnet after all. It's just that I've come to understand that some things that are devilishly hard and most distinctly *not* fun can also be very engaging and deeply satisfying when we conquer them. Similarly, I now know what it means to focus on "what matters most." Lynn Erickson's work has played a formative role for me in establishing that clarity.

Still later in my teaching, I read the work of Phil Phenix, who reminds us that human beings are born asking the question, "What is life and who am I in it?" He goes on to remind us that most of us die still trying to answer that question. The disciplines, he says, are designed to help us answer the question. History answers the question, "What is life and who am I in it?"—as do science, music, literature, and so on. I can remember with disturbing clarity my realization that Phenix was right, and that my curriculum was falling well short of helping students see that power in what we explored. The way I thought about curriculum got a rapid and very extreme makeover at that point, and the results with my students were compelling. I saw them go inside their minds and experiences in a way I'd never seen before. I watched them make links between the ideas we discussed in class and what they saw in the world around them.

It was only after I left the public school classroom and encountered Lynn Erickson's writing that I had the epiphany I'd been seeking. Lynn's work did what all good writing does when we encounter it at teachable moments in our lives. It made me say, "She understands what I tried to do, and she validates it—but more important, she gives me a vocabulary to think more precisely and more sharply about the work of curriculum design." All those years, I'd been hunting for the notion of concepts and principles and didn't know those words existed in terms of curriculum design. I'd been imprecise in distinguishing key information from key insights about a subject. Lynn broke the code for me.

Once that happened, I understood many things—or at least began to understand them. The content of my curriculum was composed of concrete facts and abstract understandings, or principles and generalizations, and skills. The facts made sense in light of the principles and generalizations. Otherwise, the facts became a grand game of trivia. The skills gave us a way to act upon the important ideas. I began to see that a worthwhile activity for students would likely ask them to use a key skill and some pivotal information to understand a generalization or principle. It was as though the curriculum stars were suddenly aligned in my head and could serve as the compass for curriculum planning I'd never quite had. I saw how to cast my students as thinkers, seekers of understanding, and creators of knowledge—not merely as absorbers, pleasure seekers, or even introspectors.

FAST FORWARD TO THE PRESENT

My concern in education now is not for the teachers who seek to help students find authenticity, meaning, and utility in what they teach. My worry is for all the pressures that cause teachers to believe they can't afford the luxury of curricula with those attributes. So many factors seem to deliver the message that curriculum must be reduced to whatever can be repeated on a machine-scoreable test. Thus curriculum becomes repetition of facts and practice of skills—too often devoid of context and meaning—and most certainly devoid of the kind of pleasure that begets motivation in the young. So what's the solution?

Clearly, teachers cannot disregard mandates for student proficiency with "the basics." A list of standards, however, is not a curriculum, nor is a textbook or a pacing guide. All those things provide us with guidance about what we must teach—but they are only the beginning of our roles as teachers. Here's an analogy for thinking about the role of standards in curriculum.

We would not invite people we care about to have dinner with us only to guide them into our kitchens and suggest that they make their way down the kitchen counter, eating raw beans in an unopened can, garlic still in its husk, raw hamburger, a pinch of salt and pepper, and so on. Those things are not dinner. They are ingredients for dinner. A cook or a chef takes the ingredients and blends them—often adding additional ingredients—to make food that is healthful and inviting.

As teachers, we can't afford to blur the lines between ingredients and dinner. We may be provided with ingredients for curriculum—but they aren't curriculum. To develop defensible curriculum, we have to use the ingredients in ways that invite students to the table of learning, in ways that contribute to strong minds, and in ways that commend learning as deeply fulfilling.

This book is a guide for making dinner—really good dinner—from raw ingredients. Lynn Erickson helps us see how facts, concepts, generalizations, and principles interrelate to reveal the meaning inherent in a subject. She helps us see how skills guide students in becoming actors on the stage of learning. She reminds us that all students deserve and need to derive meaning and power from curriculum and thus dispels the myth that only a small group of students should work with high-level, meaning-rich curriculum. She helps us see that concepts and principles are the basis for defensible differentiation—ensuring that all students work with the essential framework of meaning in a subject, but with different support systems, at different levels of sophistication, drawing on different experiences, and so on. She illustrates how concepts are portals to relevance because of their presence in our lives. She also correctly counsels us that when students understand what they learn, student achievement rises, as do the students' prospects for a productive and satisfying life in a world much more multidimensional than an answer sheet.

Lynn's work, however, is not a recipe. She pays us the compliment of believing that teachers are willing learners who inspire their students about content in proportion to their own inspiration about the content. She asks us to do hard things—and then shows us the self-efficacy that results from the doing of those things. She ignites our imagination and intellect and thus reminds us of the power we once knew to be a part of teaching and learning.

We teach young people who *will* find satisfaction in learning—either with what we teach or outside of it. We teach young people who hunger to discover the power of their minds. We teach young people who will have to solve problems their teachers cannot begin to articulate—and who will never be able to do that with a list of largely forgotten facts. We teach young people who have a critical need to make sense of the world around them. Simple as it seems—and hard as it is to master—concept-based curriculum is the best educational tool we have for addressing those needs.

I continue to learn from Lynn and to be grateful for the contribution her work continues to make to my work. I just wish I could have learned from her a long, long time ago.

—Carol Ann Tomlinson, EdD
The University of Virginia

Acknowledgments

I would like to thank the many friends and colleagues who gave me support, suggestions, and critique in the writing of this book. Faye Zucker, my editor at Corwin Press, is always there with support and suggestions for the manuscript; Dr. Lois Lanning, Dr. Leanna Isaacson, Dr. Patrick Leighton, and Lael Williams—my "think tank" friends—forced me to challenge my thinking in different subject areas and contributed their quality ideas to this book; Dr. Robert Sylwester graciously answered my questions on the brain and pointed me toward the resources I needed; Marianne Kroll, Rich Howe, and Dennis Hillmyer contributed concept-based lessons to help teachers "see" the classroom examples; David Ford jazzed up the manuscript with his brilliant cartoons that capture the bridge between children and pedagogy; and finally, thank you to Grant Wiggins, Jay McTighe, and Carol Ann Tomlinson, who share my vision for teaching and learning, and who have contributed such solid work in helping educators think out of the box.

Corwin Press gratefully acknowledges the in-depth reviews and insightful comments of the following reviewers:

Janice Fergueson, Professor, Exceptional Education, Department of Special Instructional Programs, Western Kentucky University

William Fitzhugh, Second Grade Teacher, Reisterstown Elementary School, Reisterstown, MD

Kathy Hargrove, Associate Dean, School of Education and Human Development, Southern Methodist University

Lois Lanning, Assistant Superintendent of Schools, Pomperaug Regional School District 15, Middlebury, CT

Jay McTighe, Educational Consultant, McTighe and Associates, Columbia, MD

Carol A. Tomlinson, Professor of Educational Leadership, Curry School of Education, University of Virginia

About the Author

H. Lynn Erickson is an independent consultant assisting schools and districts nationally and internationally with concept-based curriculum design. She is a recognized presenter at national conferences and is featured in the video *Planning Integrated Units: A Concept-Based Approach* (produced by the Association for Supervision and Curriculum Development) as well as in videos for Teachstream. She is the author of *Stirring the Head, Heart, and Soul: Redefining Curriculum and Instruction* (2001) and *Concept-Based Curriculum and Instruction: Teaching Beyond the Facts* (2002), by Corwin Press.

Lynn was born and raised in Fairbanks, Alaska, the daughter of a pioneering gold miner and a first-grade teacher. She graduated from the University of Alaska in 1968 and taught different grade levels in Alaska, California, and Montana. At the University of Montana, she earned master's and doctorate degrees in curriculum and instruction and advanced school administration. She worked as a Curriculum Director and School Principal for 16 years in Montana and Washington. She has been assisting elementary and secondary schools with concept-based curriculum design for the past 12 years.

She and Ken have two grown children, Kelly Cameron and Kenneth Erickson; a daughter-in-law, Jodie Erickson; and two grandsons, Trevor and Connor Cameron. They bring joy to every day. When she isn't traveling to school districts, Lynn and Ken enjoy in-line skating and motorcycling. Lynn can be reached by e-mail at hlynn@att.net.

Introduction

Complexity. In a globally interdependent world, the concept of *complexity* frames the sociopolitical and environmental issues of the day. Strongly held beliefs and values lead to increasing polarization and conflict. Competing perspectives and ideologies continuously pull in this or that direction.

Educators are charged with preparing students to live and work in this complex, interactive world. Intuitively, they realize that helping students learn to use their minds well must be a major focus for instruction. But even with this realization, they struggle with the realities of educational challenges:

♦ How can I develop the critical, creative, and conceptual minds of students and still teach the required content?
♦ How can I meet the expectations of academic standards given the time constraints and the diversity of student needs?
♦ How do I design curriculum and instruction to truly develop each student's intellect and problem-solving ability?
♦ Where can I find the time and professional training to prepare myself for the complexities of 21st-century teaching?
♦ How can I find the time to plan effectively for teaching and learning?

This book provides many answers to the questions—but it requires a mind shift in traditional ways of looking at curriculum design and pedagogy. The insights in this book are grounded in cognitive science, learning theory, and the commonsense reasoning of what works in teaching and learning. My educational journey of 38 years has provided opportunities to teach, evaluate, design, stumble, forge on, and synthesize what works in teaching and learning. For the past 18 years, I have focused my work intensively on curriculum design and instruction at all levels and in all subjects. This book shares the understandings of curriculum and instruction gleaned from my journey. These insights are not frivolous fads or fanciful musings. They are deeper insights into the inherent structure of knowledge and the relationships among curriculum design, instruction, and the development of intelligence. The following seven findings summarize the insights. The first insight is the primary focus for this book:

1. The key to intellectual development is the *synergistic interplay* between the factual and conceptual levels of thinking. Synergy refers to an interaction where the sum effect is greater than either agent acting alone. Traditional curriculum models generally fail to systematically set up this intellectual synergy. When curriculum and instruction require students to process factual information through the conceptual level of thinking, the students demonstrate greater retention of factual information, deeper levels of understanding, and increased motivation for learning.

2. Traditional curriculum design models fail to provide a strong conceptual structure for the information base. The educational result is a *coverage* curriculum model, which encourages cognitively shallow teaching and learning.

3. Every discipline has an inherent conceptual structure. As the information base expands, these conceptual structures become increasingly important for patterning, sorting, and processing incoming information.

    The greater the amount of factual information, the greater the need to rise to a higher level of abstraction to organize and process that information.

4. Though Benjamin Bloom's taxonomy of educational objectives (Bloom et al., 1956) has provided a useful tool to help students perform at different cognitive levels related to a particular topic, it does not directly address the need for students to develop conceptual understanding so they can process factual information at deeper levels and enhance knowledge retention and transfer.

5. National academic standards are *generally* incoherent in their cross-disciplinary design:
    ◆ Science standards are concept based
    ◆ Social studies standards are fact based
    ◆ Mathematics standards are skill based
    ◆ English/language arts standards are skill based

    This incoherence in design at the national level has led to an incoherence in the design of academic standards at the state level. Each disciplinary set of standards should have an overall conceptual structure, with specific content and skill standards supporting the deeper conceptual structures.

6. In addition to specific content knowledge and skills, a district curriculum needs to clearly articulate the concepts, generalizations, and principles for

each grade level and each discipline. These statements are the essential, enduring ideas that students must *understand* at a deeper level. The factual knowledge is what students must *know* in order to describe, discuss, explain, or analyze the deeper concepts. One cannot understand the conceptual level without the supporting factual knowledge. But there must be a synergy between the two levels if we are to systematically develop intelligence.

7. Educators often wonder why children enter school as eager, motivated learners but become harder to motivate as they move beyond third grade. My theory is that there is an inverse relationship between an expanding fact base through the grade levels and engagement of the child's personal, conceptual mind.

The early primary grade curriculum is far more conceptual than factual. Teachers invite children to put their minds, hearts, and hands to work in understanding concepts like colors, weather, family, fairy tales, and numbers. Children bring their personal intellect to the tasks as they collaborate, create, and problem solve. Each child feels the personal exhilaration of using his or her mind well. Joey loves to learn because he is using his own brain. But Joey moves through the grades and something happens. There is a subtle shift from engaging Joey's conceptual mind to covering the growing body of factual content. Almost imperceptibly at first, Joey begins to lose interest in learning. Teachers think it must be the action video games and sound-bite television programs that are creating the apathy in classrooms. But perhaps it is the "selling out" of personal synergistic thinking to a flatline humdrum of content coverage. As the factual load increases, the conceptual intellectual engagement and consequent motivation for learning decreases. But teachers can fix this design problem with a concept-based model for curriculum and instruction.

We have much work to do in improving education for our young people. Hurricane Katrina, which devastated several states in the southern United States in 2005, is a current example of the need for higher levels of conceptual thinking. We live in a complex age that holds the potential for massive destruction on both the environmental and sociopolitical fronts. Effective responses to complex problems require the abilities to abstract, conceptualize, predict, collaborate, plan, and act accordingly.

Teachers and administrators need significant retraining; curriculum needs to be redesigned; school districts need systems' approaches for organizational effectiveness. These are not new goals for education. They are espoused every year. But why have we not arrived? Could it be that we remain stuck in old design paradigms?

As you read the following chapters, you will compare the excitement of thinking classrooms to the dull throb of mind-numbing, "drill and kill" scenarios. You will come to understand the inherent structure of knowledge and realize the critical nature of that structure for intellectual development. You will see how to design quality instructional units and lessons for the classroom that contextualize academic standards to realize the deeper intent and to make them more manageable. You will learn how to design and teach for deeper understanding and the transfer of knowledge through a concept-based curriculum and instruction model. Finally, you will consider the leadership role in facilitating the changes outlined in this book. The change process is a journey—not an end point. Across the world, teachers and administrators are at various stages on this journey. I hope this book helps illuminate a teaching/learning path for thinking classrooms.

The Thinking Classroom

In an elementary school, the classroom buzzes with activity. Children work in small research and discussion groups, intent on discovering the answer to a question posed by the teacher: "How do simple machines increase work efficiency?" Students collaborate as they hypothesize and design and carry out experiments using levers, pulleys, and ramps. The teacher asks the students to use the concepts of *force* and *energy* to describe the results of their experiments. Students express ideas, question each other, and extend their thinking. New understandings emerge and are recorded in sentences next to drawings of their simple machines. A visual scan of the classroom confirms an active learning environment. Student work lines the walls, and books, art prints, science materials, mathematics manipulatives, and computers are evident in the plentiful workspace.

In a secondary school, students use desktop computers and access databases to find relevant material on global pollution. They process the information through the conceptual lens of *environmental sustainability* as they think beyond the facts. They compare notes with students around the world, and design PowerPoint programs to display their research and deepening understanding of global pollution and sustainability. They scan in pictures to enhance the graphic appeal. These are the students of the computer age, and they produce a score of intellectual, artistic, and informative products.

Down the hall in another classroom, students sit placidly in rows and stare at their textbooks while child after child reads a paragraph. Behind the vacant eyes, minds are playing—outside. The teacher controls the scene from a stool in the front of the room and questions the facts just read. Posters hang on the wall like soldiers at attention, and books sit in tidy positions on the shelves, sorted by size. The room is quiet except for the bored drone of the student reading and the interminable tick of a clock on the teacher's desk.

The art and science of teaching go beyond the presentation of information. Artful teachers engage students emotionally, creatively, and intellectually to instill deep and passionate curiosity in learning. They know how to effectively use the structures offered by the science of teaching to facilitate the personal construction of knowledge. But the personal construction of knowledge is not "whatever." The teachers are clear on what they want their students to know factually, understand conceptually, and be able to do in skills and processes.

What may appear to the casual observer as ill-structured activity in a classroom is actually goal-oriented learning. The teacher has artfully designed the lesson with questions and experiences so that students are building and sharing disciplinary knowledge and understanding aligned to academic standards. The learning is purposeful. But the teacher also designs for learning to encourage the discovery of unintended insights and understandings. The discussion of essential questions, inquiry-based learning, and the encouragement to make meaning and express ideas through art supports this extension. Intellectual development, mindful learning, and creative expression are key instructional goals.

Mr. Howe is a middle school social studies teacher. He has been teaching about early American colonization and wants his students to internalize an enduring understanding of history—that *developing nations may resist or revolt against a ruling country's social, economic, and political policies if they are perceived as unjust.* He developed the following lesson to help students internalize facts supporting this understanding.

> You are a creative designer for Gameboards USA. You have been charged by the president of the company with designing a game to teach fifth graders about the reasons leading up to the American Revolution. Your game must have questions that address the social, political, and economic conflicts between England and the settled colonies.

To assess the students' factual knowledge on reasons for the American Revolution, Mr. Howe gave a selected response test. As an extension assignment, Mr. Howe asked students to research the causes of two other political revolutions in history (students chose their revolutions from a teacher-supplied list). Then he assessed their conceptual understanding that *people may revolt against governmental policies that are perceived as oppressive or unjust* through the following task:

> You have studied the causes of the American Revolution and two other political revolutions in history. Working in a cooperative group, create a graphic organizer that compares the causes of the three revolutions. As a group, determine one common factor that led to revolution across the three examples. Individually, choose one of the following formats and illustrate that common factor:
>
> ♦ Political cartoon
> ♦ Newspaper article
> ♦ Poster
> ♦ Poem

Thinking classrooms employ concept-based curriculum and instruction design models. These models are inherently more sophisticated than traditional models because they are as concerned with intellectual development as they are with gaining knowledge.

Concept-based curricular and instructional designs are *three-dimensional*—that is, curriculum and instruction is focused on what students will . . .

♦ *K*now (factually),
♦ *U*nderstand (conceptually), and
♦ be able to *D*o (skillfully).

SOURCE: David Ford Cartoons, davidford@ cablespeed.com. Used with permission.

Traditionally, curriculum and instruction has been more *two-dimensional* in design (know and able to do)—resting on a misguided assumption that knowing facts is evidence of deeper, conceptual understanding.

The following performance indicators, for example, are typical expectations across state history standards:

♦ Identify economic differences among different regions of the United States.
♦ Compare changes in technology (past to present).

These performance indicators are written in the traditional format of content "objectives," with a verb followed by the topic. It is assumed that the ability to carry out these objectives is evidence of understanding; but, as written, they fail to take students to the third dimension of *conceptual understanding* where the deeper lessons of history reside. Students will research and memorize facts about the economic differences in regions of the United States, but the thinking stops there. Try this task to reach the third dimension. Complete the sentences by extrapolating transferable understandings (timeless ideas supported by the factual content):

♦ Identify economic differences among different regions of the United States *in order to understand that . . .*
♦ Compare changes in technology (past to present) *in order to understand that . . .*

What do you think the writers of these performance indicators for middle school expected students to understand at a level beyond the facts? Below are some possible endings:

♦ Identify economic differences among different regions of the United States *in order to understand that the geography and natural resources of a region shape the economy.*
♦ Compare changes in technology *in order to understand that advancing technologies change the social and economic patterns of a society.*

We cannot just assume that teachers reach the conceptual level of understanding with students. In fact, years of work facilitating the writing of these essential, enduring understandings with teachers has shown me that it is a skill that takes practice. Extrapolating deeper understandings from factual knowledge is not easy work. It involves thinking beyond the facts to the "So what?"—the significant and transferable understandings. It involves mentally manipulating language and syntax so that conceptual understandings are expressed with clarity, brevity, and power. Teachers across the board say, "This is hard work!" when they begin this writing process. The learning curve is steep, but with a little practice, teachers take pride in their finely honed understandings.

Becoming a three-dimensional, concept-based teacher is a journey that merges best practices in teaching and learning with a developing understanding of brain-based pedagogy. But we have much to learn. So let's get on with the journey.

THE BRAIN AT WORK

The cognitive sciences have produced prolific writers on the anatomy and functioning of the brain (Calvin, 1996; Calvin & Ojemann, 1994; Mandler, 2004) and on the implications for teaching and learning (Gardner, 1999; Novak & Gowin, 1999; Ritchart, 2002; Sousa, 2001; Sternberg, 2002; Sylwester, 2003; Wolfe, 2001).

At the cellular level, the brain is composed of billions of neurons and trillions of glial support cells. Robert Sylwester (2003) describes the brain's macrocomposition as a subcortical area consisting of the brain stem and surrounding systems with "pea- to walnut-shaped modular structures" that control basic brain processes governing survival and emotional needs. Above the subcortical area is the cortex. Sylwester (2003, p. 20) describes the cortex as a "six layer sheet of deeply folded neural tissue . . . that encompasses 85% of our brain, and processes learned rational logical behaviors."

The sensory lobes process relevant incoming sensory information and integrate it into a unified perceptual field. This analysis is then relayed to the frontal lobes for evaluation and action. Pat Wolfe, in *Brain Matters* (2001, p. 42), states, "Our human cortex allows us to build cathedrals, compose symphonies, dream and plan for a better future, love, hate, and experience emotional pain, because it is in the cortex that consciousness—our ability to be aware of what we are thinking, feeling, and doing—emerges."

Other books devoted to the structure and function of the brain provide detailed information related to other parts of the brain, such as the thalamus and hypothalamus, and describe the neural communication process across synaptic divides (Sousa, 2001; Sylwester, 2003, 2005; Wolfe, 2001). But since the focus of this book is developing intelligence through conceptual thinking, a primary function of the cerebral cortex, we will leave the remaining details on the structure and function of the brain to other authors.

It is important to this book, however, to share and affirm an observation by Sylwester (2003, p. 23): "We're used to thinking of intelligence as something that occurs entirely within our brain, but this is now seen as a very narrow view of a complex process that also involves our body and the environment in which our body-brain functions." How true! Intelligence does not operate in a vacuum. Our senses, emotions, physical involvement, and environmental context all play a critical role in the development of intelligence.

SYNERGISTIC THINKING

As a career educator who has climbed peaks and fallen into valleys in my work over the years, I now realize some of the major reasons that children do not retain, transfer, and understand knowledge as well as they should—in spite of the dedicated and tireless efforts of teachers to teach and reteach year after year. Perhaps the most significant reason that children overall are not performing as well as they should academically is that we provide teachers with intellectually shallow curriculum materials that fail to engage higher-order thinking. Let me explain.

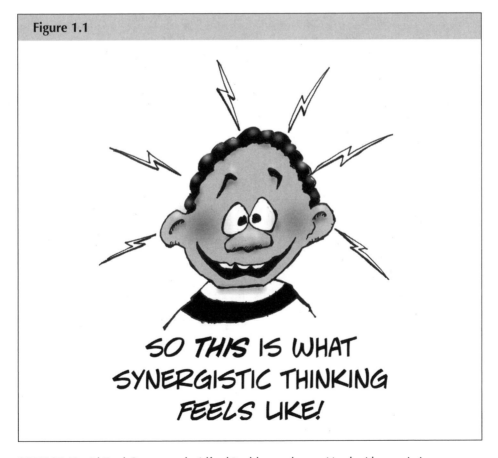

Figure 1.1

SOURCE: David Ford Cartoons, davidford@cablespeed.com. Used with permission.

To memorize information is lower-level cognitive work. To stimulate more sophisticated, complex thinking, we need to create a *synergy* between the simpler and more complex processing centers in the brain. This interactive synergy requires the mind to process information on two cognitive levels—the factual and the conceptual. The conceptual mind uses facts as a tool to discern patterns, connections, and deeper, transferable understandings.

But curriculum materials are seldom designed to systematically set up this intellectual synergy between the factual and conceptual levels of thinking. Though concepts are mentioned, and often defined, they appear to be "Oh, by the way . . ." afterthoughts that one might want to consider. To provide teachers with a specific strategy for creating this intellectual synergy, the next section discusses and demonstrates the use of a *conceptual lens* in curriculum design and instruction.

The Power of a Conceptual Lens

Concept-based teachers know how to adapt lower-level curriculum materials to teach for deeper understanding. For example, they may use a conceptual lens to invite students to bring their own thinking to the study at hand. Janet Kaduce is teaching a unit on the Holocaust in her high school class. She invites students to consider the events in terms of the dual conceptual lens of *humanity/inhumanity*.

This lens is the vehicle that sets up a synergy between the factual and conceptual processing centers in the brain. Students think deeply because they must process the facts in terms of their relationship to the ideas of *humanity* and *inhumanity*.

The teacher uses different types of questions to extend student thinking and deepen understanding:

Factual Questions:

Why was the Holocaust a significant event in world history?

What beliefs did Hitler hold that drove his actions?

Why is Hitler's persecution of the Jewish people considered inhumane?

Conceptual Questions:

What examples of inhumanity can you cite from our world today?

What acts of humanity can you cite from our present-day world?

How are beliefs, values, and perspectives related to views of humanity and inhumanity?

Provocative (Debate, or Essential) Question:

Can one be inhumane and civilized at the same time? (Explain your answer.)

Students retain the factual information longer because the use of the conceptual lens requires them to intellectually process at a deeper level. Furthermore, because students are invited to bring their own thinking to the factual study, they are better able to make personal meaning. This invitation involves them emotionally—they are personally invested—and the motivation for learning increases.

Figure 1.2 provides a list of potential conceptual lenses that teachers could use to engage a student's conceptual mind. The focus a teacher wishes to bring to a study suggests a particular lens, so it is best to start with the topic and then select the lens. There are times, however, such as in literature study, when a teacher might begin with a lens, such as *tragedy* or *archetypes*, and then select the support material, but generally the link is stronger if the topic is considered first. Notice that some of the lenses in Figure 1.2 are very broad (macroconcepts), such as *system* or *change*; while others are more specific (microconcepts), such as *identity* or *heroes*. A more specific lens reflects the teacher's particular conceptual focus. As a general rule, discipline-based studies (e.g., a literature unit) draw more on the specific lenses; interdisciplinary studies draw on the broader lenses because they can then be accessed by a variety of disciplines involved in the study.

Try this activity to experience the power of the conceptual lens:

1. Think of two specific topics from a curriculum you teach.

2. Choose potential lenses from the list in Figure 1.2 for each topic.

   Notice how the lens changes the focus for thinking about the topic.

   Which lens do you find most engaging (or challenging) for your topic?

   Thinking reflectively (metacognitively), are you aware of how the lens invites you to bring your personal intellect to the study? Does the engagement of your personal intellect increase your motivation and interest in this study?

   Topics   *Potential Lenses*

   A. _____   _____

                                         _____

                                         _____

   B. _____   _____

                                         _____

                                         _____

The Integration of Thinking

When we can rise above the facts and see the patterns and connections between the facts and related concepts, principles, and generalizations—and when we can understand the deeper, transferable significance of knowledge—then we can say our thinking is *integrated* at a conceptual level. This factual/conceptual integration of thinking should be a conscious design goal for curriculum and instruction.

Figure 1.2	Sample Conceptual Lenses
Conflict	Complexity
Beliefs/Values	Paradox
Interdependence	Interactions
Freedom	Transformations
Identity	Patterns
Relationships	Origins
Change	Revolution
Perspective	Reform
Power	Influence
System	Balance
Structure/Function	Innovation
Design	Genius
Heroes	Utility
Force	Creativity

I view integration as a cognitive process rather than what we do with subjects. Under this view, integration can occur in inter- and intradisciplinary contexts as long as there is a conceptual lens or focus that pulls thinking to the integration level—where patterns and connections are made between the factual and conceptual levels of knowledge.

This integration of thinking allows knowledge to be transferred. For example, the lens of *beliefs and values* can provide intellectual focus to a unit on "The Iraq War" and be the invitation for students to use their own minds to think more deeply. The deeper thinking on the complexities of war leads to lessons of history that can be transferred through time and across situations.

In addition to using a conceptual lens to integrate thinking, teaching inductively to conceptual ideas (generalizations and principles) also facilitates the integration of thinking. These conceptual ideas are commonly referred to as "enduring understandings" (Wiggins & McTighe, 1999), "essential understandings" (Erickson, 1995), or "big ideas" in today's education jargon.

The enduring understanding that "artists often use a combination of color harmonies to create emotional complexity" is not just an empty idea in art education. It is a synthesis of thought and conceptual understanding supported by concrete

Figure 1.3

SOURCE: David Ford Cartoons, davidford@cablespeed.com. Used with permission.

examples—from the bold and vibrant colors of a Matisse still life, which reflect assertiveness and joy, to the muted tones of a Picasso blue period. Chapter 2, "The Structure of Knowledge," will discuss conceptual understanding in greater depth, stressing the significance for teaching, learning, and intellectual development.

The Transfer of Knowledge

The ability to transfer knowledge and skills to new or similar contexts is evidence of deeper understanding and higher-order thinking. Because the coverage model of curriculum design values memorization over the integration of thinking and the transfer of knowledge, these higher-order processes may appear to teachers as serendipitous displays of student genius when they bolt out of the classroom blue. Teachers eagerly e-mail a colleague, "You wouldn't believe the insight and thinking that came out of Robert and Kim today when we were discussing the global issue of overpopulation!"

Yet integrated thinking and the transfer of knowledge should be daily fare in classrooms. *Making meaning* is not simply doing hands-on activities related to a topic, or learning the meaning of vocabulary words. Making meaning includes the interplay of lower- and higher-order thinking. This means that the design of curriculum and instruction needs to set up this interplay.

> Curriculum and instruction models that set up a synergistic interplay between the factual and conceptual levels of thinking are critical to intellectual development. The sophistication of the intellectual dance across synaptic divides in the brain determines the quality of the performance. As educators, we are responsible for the design of the dance.

Richard Paul (Foundation for Critical Thinking) wrote a paper titled "Making Critical Thinking Intuitive" and stated that "intuitive understanding enables [us] to insightfully bridge the gap between an abstract concept and concrete applications" (1995a, p. 2). He calls on all levels of education to teach in a way that fosters intuitive understanding. Paul states,

> If we focused attention, as we should, on the ability of students to move back and forth comfortably and insightfully between the abstract and the concrete, they would soon develop and discipline their imaginations . . . to generate cases that exemplify abstractions. All students have, as a matter of fact, experienced hundreds of situations that exemplify any number of important abstract truths and principles. But they are virtually never asked to dig into their experience to find examples, to imagine cases, which illustrate this or that principle, this or that abstract concept. The result is an undisciplined and underdeveloped imagination combined with vague, indeed muddled, concepts and principles. . . . What is missing is the intuitive synthesis between concept and percept, between idea and experience, between image and reality. (1995, p. 17)

I agree with Paul that there is a lack of intuitive synthesis in teaching and learning. Intuitive synthesis would be an important component in what I refer to as the "integration of thinking." But I don't believe the problem starts with teachers. It is a muddled curriculum design that nurtures muddled thinking. Teachers want to do their very best work. They spend many hours of their own time planning and preparing for instruction. But the reality is that we continue to provide low-level curricular materials and weak training in sound pedagogy. Some teachers overcome these realities by redesigning lessons and taking charge of their own staff development. But these teachers are not the norm. We must address the rest.

DEVELOPING THE INTELLECT

Intellectual Character

Schools play a critical role in the development of the intellect. But as Ron Ritchart, in *Intellectual Character* (2002), so aptly observes,

School . . . [is more about] style than substance, breadth than depth, and speed above all else (p. xxi). We've come to mistake curriculums, textbooks, standards, objectives, and tests as ends in themselves rather than as means to an end. (p. 8)

Ritchart cautions that we are teaching for the wrong thing—that we need to keep our focus on the development of "intellectual dispositions" that develop strong "intellectual character" (2002, p. 10). Ritchart defines *intellectual character* as the "patterns" of behavior, thinking, and interaction that are shaped and exhibited over time (p. 9). He frames the idea of *intellectual dispositions* under the categories of creative thinking (open-minded, curious), critical thinking (seeking truth and understanding, strategic, skeptical), and reflective thinking (metacognitive) (p. 27).

Many educators feel that the pressure to meet academic standards necessitates coverage and speed, and that there is not enough time to develop "intellectual character." But let's not lose sight of the purpose of education. It has to be more than obtaining a fund of information or learning sets of discrete skills. Indeed, the survival of a society depends on its ability to respond intelligently and creatively to social, economic, political, and environmental problems. Information without intellect is meaningless.

We can meet the intent of standards and still keep our focus on intellectual development. The secret is in the design of curriculum and instruction—and in the willingness of the teacher to learn and practice strategies that develop intellectual dispositions. Three-dimensional, concept-based curriculum and instruction provide a powerful frame for the development of these intellectual dispositions.

Creative Thinking

Ritchart states that the dispositions of open-mindedness and curiosity are components of creative thinking (2002, p. 28). Open-mindedness depends on the ability to reflect critically on incoming information, consider and "play" with alternative points of view, and intuitively and flexibly look for patterns and connections between elements. Curiosity drives the development of intelligence. It is the "on" switch for learning, and the gateway to creative problem solving.

The role of emotional engagement in learning has been well documented in recent years (Sousa, 2001; Sylwester, 2003; Wolfe, 2001). We retain knowledge longer and gain deeper understanding when there is an emotional response to learning. This, too, is an important point to remember when designing curriculum and instruction. Creative thinking and learning generate an emotional response because they tap the personal connection to experience.

It is interesting that Anderson and Krathwohl, in *A Taxonomy for Learning, Teaching, and Assessing: A Revision of Bloom's Taxonomy of Educational Objectives* (2001, p. 68), changed the term for Benjamin Bloom's cognitive process of "synthesis" to "creativity" and moved it to the highest level of intellectual functioning. This change makes sense—because the ability to create requires the production of an original or unique product or idea generated from the synthesis and creative extension of discrete elements.

SOURCE: David Ford Cartoons, davidford@cablespeed.com. Used with permission.

The area of creative thinking fascinates me because it is the ultimate expression of reflective and critical thinking. Creative thinking becomes increasingly important in a world dealing with complex problems. Daniel H. Pink, a writer, lecturer, and international observer of economic and social trends, wrote an interesting book titled *A Whole New Mind: Moving From the Information Age to the Conceptual Age* (2005). His opening paragraph:

The last few decades have belonged to a certain kind of person with a certain kind of mind—computer programmers who could crack code, lawyers who could craft contracts, MBAs who could crunch numbers. But the keys to the kingdom are changing hands. The future belongs to a very different kind of person with a very different kind of mind—creators and empathizers, pattern recognizers, and meaning makers. These people—artists, inventors, designers, storytellers, caregivers, consolers, big picture thinkers—will now reap society's richest rewards and share its greatest joys. (p. 1)

Hmmm. This is an interesting observation. Pink further states,

The wealth of nations and the well-being of individuals now depend on having artists in the room. In a world enriched by abundance but disrupted by the automation and outsourcing of white-collar work, everyone, regardless of profession, must cultivate an artistic sensibility. . . . Today we must all be designers. (p. 69)

Pink is not implying that we no longer need linear, logical, and deductive thinkers; but he is highlighting the increasing importance of creative thinking to solve increasingly complex problems and to enhance daily lives.

The August 2005 report on "Getting Smarter, Becoming Fairer," by the Center for American Progress and the Institute for America's Future, reported that in 2001, 47 percent of U.S. patents went to foreign inventors. Though American citizens received the most patents, they were followed closely by Japanese citizens. Japan, China, and India have each more than tripled their U.S. patent awards since 1991 (2005, p. 10). The innovative and creative edge that the United States has long relied on is facing strong competition today.

Though all disciplines benefit from the use of creative thinking in problem solving, it is a wellspring for the arts. It is alarming to see schools cutting out art programs to make more time for standards drill and kill. Science helps people understand and explain phenomena in the natural and constructed world. Art goes a step further and allows one to create and share a personal interpretation of the physical and sociocultural world.

Creative thinking is the personal construction of *meaning*. Creative thinking employs imagination and playful tinkering with shapes, sounds, colors, words, and ideas. Creative thinking is the birthplace for unique and innovative products, cultural expressions, and solutions to global problems.

Of all the disciplines, art is the most open-ended. Though it has a formal structure of concepts and principles that provide the language of the craft and critique, art stimulates the creative mind more than any other discipline. The creative mind develops cognitive flexibility; can examine situations, objects, and issues from multiple perspectives; and can propose novel solutions to persistent problems. So even though art has intrinsic value as a personal and social expression of culture and emotion, it has heightened importance today as a powerful vehicle for developing creative thinking. The future of our world depends on the marriage of creative, critical, conceptual, and reflective thinking. No doubt about it.

Figure 1.5

SOURCE: David Ford Cartoons, davidford@cablespeed.com. Used with permission.

Critical Thinking

Ritchart (2002, p. 29) includes the dispositions of "seeking truth and understanding, being strategic, and being skeptical" as components of critical thinking. Citizens today are inundated with multiple perspectives and opinions that may or may not be supported by facts. Critical thinkers open-mindedly evaluate incoming information by determining the basis and validity for the views being expressed. They maintain a healthy skepticism toward the information until all the facts are in. They are aware of the times when they are interjecting their personal bias into the evaluation of a situation, and attempt to hold their bias in check as they consider the evidence. Critical thinkers use logic to solve problems. They strategically plan for dealing with the issue by clarifying the problem and its components, by considering the viability of alternative solutions, and by laying out a time line and set of steps to achieve resolution.

Richard Paul and Linda Elder, the director of research and the president, respectively, of the Foundation for Critical Thinking, have contributed greatly to our understanding of critical thinking. I highly recommend the set of 15 "Thinker's Guides" sold through the foundation (www.criticalthinking.org). These guides are based on decades of research (and critical thinking) by Paul and Elder. In one of these booklets, *The Miniature Guide to Critical Thinking Concepts and Tools* (2004b, p. 1), Paul and Elder provide a helpful definition:

> Critical thinking is a process by which the thinker improves the quality of his or her thinking by skillfully taking charge of the structures inherent in thinking and imposing intellectual standards upon them. Critical thinking is, in short, self-directed, self-disciplined, self-monitored, and self-corrective thinking.

Reflective (Metacognitive) Thinking

One of the greatest contributions Paul and Elder have made to the area of critical thinking is a set of intellectual standards. The journey of conceptual thinking, as well as the other kinds of critical thinking, requires ongoing metacognitive work. Intellectual standards and questions (Figure 1.6) provided by Paul and Elder in *The Thinker's Guide to the Nature and Function of Critical and Creative Thinking* aid this metacognitive work (2004a, p. 26).

In *The Logic of Creative and Critical Thinking* (1995b, p. 1), Richard Paul discusses the symbiotic relationship between critical and creative thinking. He suggests that excellent thinking results in creative ends—"designing or engendering, fashioning or originating, creating or producing . . . ," but to achieve these ends there must be continual metacognitive assessment of our thinking—"is it on-track and sufficiently clear, accurate, precise, consistent, relevant, deep, or broad for the end goals? In other words, creativity and criticality [are] interwoven into one seamless fabric" (p. 2).

Metacognitive assessment of thinking needs intellectual standards. Teachers can use the work of Paul and Elder to help students reflect on the quality and progress of their thinking abilities. We have so much work to do in the area of metacognition. These intellectual standards are a solid starting point.

Conceptual Thinking

Though Ritchart and Paul do not single out the area of conceptual thinking in their discussions of intellectual work, it is a recognized form of thinking that includes aspects of critical, creative, and metacognitive thinking. Conceptual thinking requires the ability to critically examine factual information; relate to prior knowledge; see patterns and connections; draw out significant understandings at the conceptual level; evaluate the truth of the understandings based on the supporting evidence; transfer the understanding across time or situation; and, often, use the conceptual understanding to creatively solve a problem or create a new product, process, or idea. This book is dedicated to helping educators understand the nature of conceptual thinking, its importance to the overall development of the intellect generally, and how to adapt curriculum and instruction to develop this complex form of thinking.

Figure 1.6   Intellectual Standards and Focus Questions

Standard	Focus Questions
Clarity	Could you elaborate further? Could you give me an example? Could you illustrate what you mean?
Accuracy	How could we check on that? How could we find out if that is true? How could we verify or test that?
Precision	Could you be more specific? Could you give me more details? Could you be more exact?
Relevance	How does that relate to the problem? How does that bear on the question? How does that help us with the issue?
Depth	What factors make this a difficult problem? What are some of the complexities of this question? What are some of the difficulties we need to deal with?
Breadth	Do we need to look at this from another perspective? Do we need to consider another point of view? Do we need to look at this in other ways?
Logic	Does all this make sense together? Does your first paragraph fit in with your last? Does what you say follow from the evidence?
Significance	Is this the most important problem to consider? Is this the central idea to focus on? Which of these facts are most important?
Fairness	Do I have any vested interest in this issue? Am I sympathetically representing the viewpoints of others?

SOURCE: Paul, R. W., and Elder, Linda. (2004). *The Thinker's Guide to the Nature and Functions of Critical and Creative Thinking*. Santa Rosa, CA: Foundation for Critical Thinking. www.criticalthinking.org. Used with permission.

DISCIPLINARY WAYS OF THINKING AND DOING

The chapter to this point has discussed different kinds of thinking in general terms, but each discipline (art, mathematics, etc.) draws on its own unique processes, tools, and approaches to making meaning. My good friend and colleague Lael Williams and I have had many discussions on the importance of disciplinary depth for quality problem solving. My work with concept-based curriculum and instruction has emphasized the importance of systematically building conceptual knowledge, understanding, and processes/skills *by discipline* through the grades. Lael agrees—"Patterns of behavior, thinking, and interacting derive from the deep and personal experiences with disciplinary ways of knowing and doing over time." The artist, scientist, mathematician, and social scientist view and approach problems to solve in ways that are consistent with the essence of their discipline.

Lael advocates the design of curriculum and instruction that gives students the experience of being "practitioners" in a discipline. This means going beyond the teaching of content in a subject area. It means that the teacher becomes familiar with the disciplinary ways of knowing, understanding, and doing so they can design learning experiences that develop these unique approaches to problem solving and insight. This does not mean that students should always learn in disciplinary "boxes." On the contrary, examining problems and issues through *interdisciplinary* perspectives gives breadth and depth to understanding. But the reality is that interdisciplinary work is only as strong as the content, concepts, and approaches of the various disciplines brought into the study. So our suggestion to curriculum developers and teachers is this—develop disciplinary ways of knowing, understanding, and doing systematically through the grades, but engage students in complex problems to solve, or issues to understand, that encourage the flexible use of disciplinary knowledge and processes in interdisciplinary studies.

THINKING TEACHERS AND STUDENTS

If a major goal is the development of student intellect, then the importance of the teacher's ability to think critically, reflectively, creatively, and conceptually goes without question. It has been rewarding to observe teachers in concept-based workshops as they think beyond the facts in their subject area and grapple with the "so what" of why they teach particular content. The common refrain at the end of the workshop is, "My head hurts from thinking so hard!" But they also say they can hardly wait to get back to the classroom and apply what they have learned. At first, I wondered why teachers showed so much enthusiasm in workshops after expressing how hard it was to think. And then it struck me—humans are intellectual beings; we are made to think. And when we are successful in using our minds well, we feel intelligent—and are motivated to learn more. This important premise applies to students as well. They feel personal satisfaction from using their minds well.

Sometimes teachers enter the workshops eager to learn, and feel validated for the concept-based pedagogy they already practice. But they gain even deeper understandings and expand their skills as they journey forward. Other teachers may enter the workshop with negative preconceived notions; but when they see that facts are still valued as critical elements in the broader intellectual scheme, they relax and put their minds to work. Some teachers enter with trepidation because they fear they won't be able to grasp the ideas being presented. But these teachers usually leave with the comment, "I have to think more about concept-based teaching—but I know I can do this!"

Motivating students to think is a major focus for thinking teachers. They understand why society is so concerned that our students learn to think critically, reflectively, creatively, and conceptually. The August 2005 report on renewing our nation's schools (Center for American Progress/Institute for America's Future, p. 10) provides alarming statistics cited in the journal *Foreign Policy* (November–December 2004)—"only 1.6% of 24-year-olds in the United States have a bachelor's degree in engineering, compared to figures roughly two times higher in Russia, three times higher in China, and four times higher in South Korea and Japan." Further, the National Intelligence Council, in *Mapping the Global Future* (2004), states that the number of American engineering graduates has declined 20 percent since 1981, and the percentage of United States undergraduates taking engineering is the second from the lowest of all developed countries. It is apparent that the outsourcing of jobs is moving far beyond the low-skill positions. We truly are in a globally competitive job environment.

SUMMARY

This chapter on "The Thinking Classroom" is a reminder that intellectual development has to be a major educational focus if we are to prepare our young people for the complexities of 21st-century living. Thinking classrooms look different and sound different. Teachers in thinking classrooms understand how to use concepts to *integrate* student thinking at a deeper level of understanding—a level where knowledge can be transferred to other situations and times.

This chapter provides a very brief description of how the brain works and describes the power of a conceptual lens to create a synergy between the factual and conceptual levels of thinking. A chapter that is concerned with the development of thinking also values the idea of intellectual standards, as described by Richard Paul and Linda Elder, to help students metacognitively assess the quality of their thought processes. Ron Ritchart's ideas on "intellectual dispositions" pull together perspectives on critical, creative, and reflective thinking. And finally, we are reminded that intellectual dispositions gain breadth and depth when they are developed through disciplinary ways of knowing and doing and are given wings in interdisciplinary as well as intradisciplinary contexts.

Chapter 2 extends the understanding of simple and complex thinking by showing how knowledge is structured and by illustrating the difference between the factual and conceptual levels of knowledge, thinking, and understanding.

EXTENDING THOUGHT

1. How would you describe your classroom? Try writing a "classroom snapshot."

2. Would you consider your classroom concept based? Why or why not?

3. How many reasons can you think of to support concept-based curriculum and instruction?

4. How did this chapter relate synergistic thinking to the factual and conceptual levels of the mind?

5. Why does this chapter consider integration a higher-order cognitive function?

6. How does a conceptual lens facilitate the integration of thinking?

7. Why is the conceptual transfer of knowledge a key indicator of deeper understanding?

8. How would you compare education framed by the ideal of intellectual character and dispositions and education framed by a set of academic standards to cover? How can you meet the intent of academic standards without sacrificing the development of intellectual character?

9. How can students' use of intellectual standards (accuracy, clarity, relevance, depth, etc.) improve their reflective (metacognitive) thinking?

The Structure of Knowledge

THE INHERENT STRUCTURE OF KNOWLEDGE

Knowledge has an inherent structure just as the animal and plant kingdoms have a structure. In fact, all systems have an inherent structure. Without structure, differences are ill defined. An amoeba and a chimpanzee would both be classed as animals—not very helpful when one is trying to understand more specific similarities, differences, and relationships.

For my learning, Hilda Taba, a powerful and insightful educator of the 1950s and 1960s, provided a clear explanation of the different levels of knowledge abstraction and organization. She advocated teaching to the deeper understanding of concepts and *main ideas* (transferable, conceptual understandings), rather than focusing solely on a superficial coverage of factual information (Taba, 1966).

This chapter is devoted to the structure of knowledge for a number of reasons:

♦ The design of quality curriculum and instruction requires an understanding of the different levels in the structure of knowledge and the interplay of those levels in curriculum design, teaching, and learning.

♦ Teacher training institutions can better prepare teachers for the classroom by ensuring a basic understanding of how knowledge is structured and the relationship of this structure to teaching, learning, and intellectual development.

♦ State and local academic standards, as well as textbooks and other curriculum materials, can raise the intellectual bar for students and teachers by shifting from traditional lists of verb-driven objectives to clear statements of what students must *know* (critical factual knowledge), *understand* (generalizations and principles), and be able to *do* (processes/skills). Science and economics are two areas that strive to reach the conceptual levels of understanding, but history, mathematics, and most other subject areas just aren't there yet in their curriculum designs. Figure 2.1 is a visual representation of the Structure of Knowledge (Erickson, 1995, p. 68; 2001, p. 26; 2002, p. 5).

Figure 2.1   Structure of Knowledge

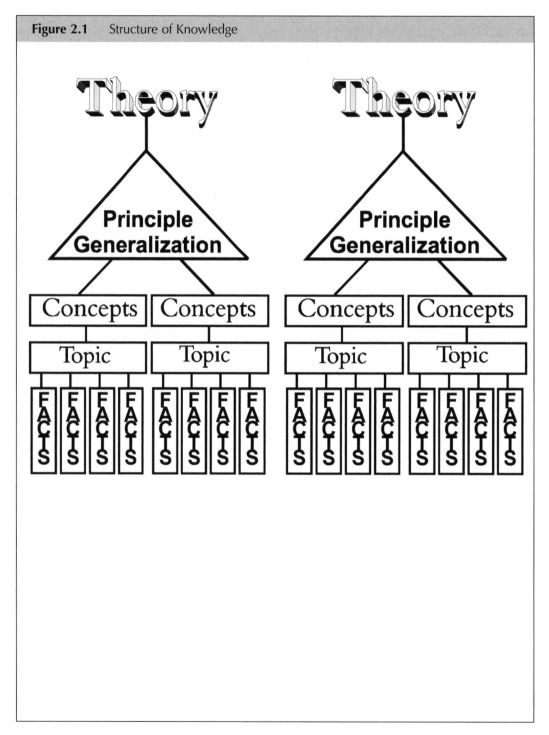

SOURCE: © 2007 by H. Lynn Erickson, *Concept-Based Curriculum and Instruction for the Thinking Classroom*. Also shown in Erickson 1995, 2001, 2002.

Figures 2.2a–f show discipline-based examples of the different levels in the Structure of Knowledge. Study the examples and see if you can articulate the difference between a *topic* and a *concept,* and the difference between a *fact* and a *generalization.*

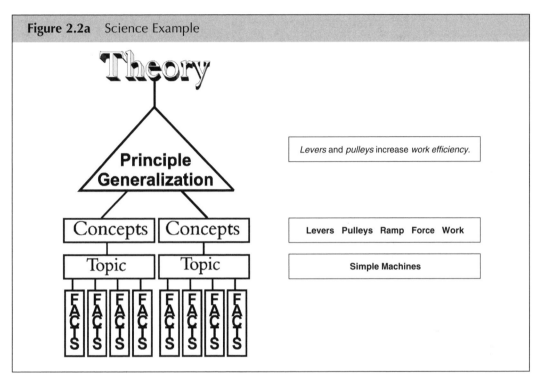

Figure 2.2a Science Example

Levers and pulleys increase work efficiency.

Levers Pulleys Ramp Force Work

Simple Machines

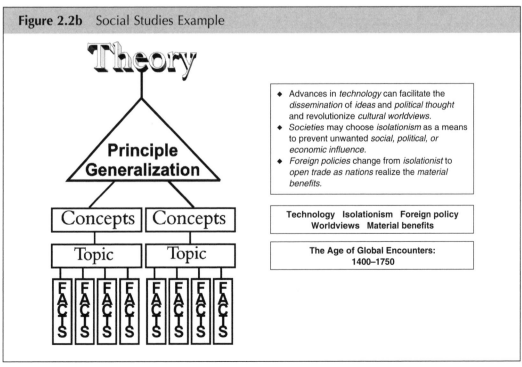

Figure 2.2b Social Studies Example

◆ Advances in *technology* can facilitate the *dissemination* of *ideas* and *political thought* and revolutionize *cultural worldviews.*
◆ *Societies* may choose *isolationism* as a means to prevent unwanted *social, political,* or *economic influence.*
◆ *Foreign policies* change from *isolationist* to *open trade as nations* realize the *material benefits.*

Technology Isolationism Foreign policy
Worldviews Material benefits

The Age of Global Encounters:
1400–1750

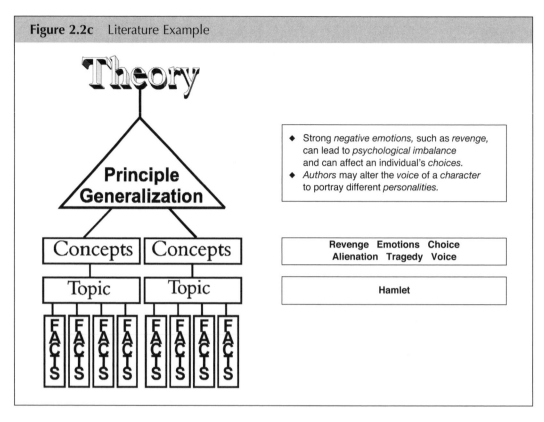

Figure 2.2c Literature Example

◆ Strong *negative emotions,* such as *revenge,* can lead to *psychological imbalance* and can affect an individual's *choices.*
◆ *Authors* may alter the *voice* of a *character* to portray different *personalities.*

Revenge Emotions Choice
Alienation Tragedy Voice

Hamlet

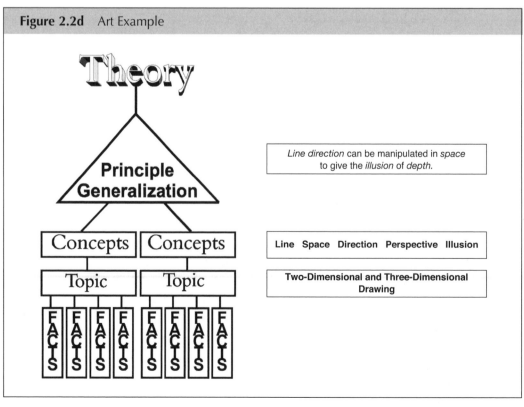

Figure 2.2d Art Example

Line direction can be manipulated in *space* to give the *illusion* of *depth.*

Line Space Direction Perspective Illusion

Two-Dimensional and Three-Dimensional Drawing

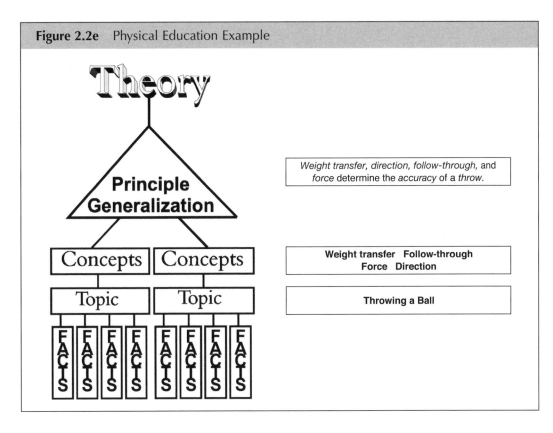

Figure 2.2e Physical Education Example

Weight transfer, direction, follow-through, and *force* determine the *accuracy* of a *throw.*

Weight transfer   Follow-through
Force   Direction

Throwing a Ball

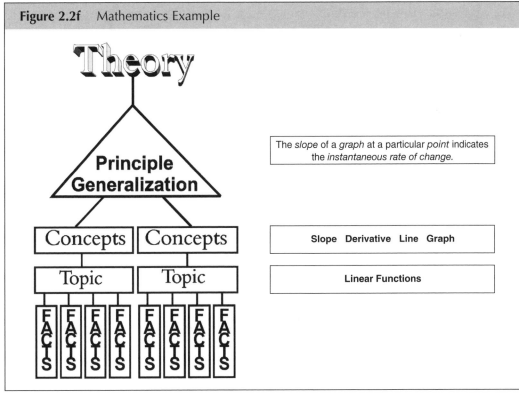

Figure 2.2f Mathematics Example

The *slope* of a *graph* at a particular *point* indicates the *instantaneous rate of change.*

Slope   Derivative   Line   Graph

Linear Functions

Note on Topics and Concepts in Mathematics

In mathematics, the Structure of Knowledge is much more conceptual than in topic-heavy disciplines like history. So when mathematics teachers think of their organizing topic, they are actually identifying a broader organizing concept (see "Linear Functions" example in Figure 2.2f). The reason mathematics is structured differently from history is that mathematics is an inherently conceptual language of concepts, subconcepts, and their relationships. Number, pattern, measurement, statistics, and so on are the broadest conceptual organizers. Under each of these macroconcepts are the subconcepts. For example, the macroconcept of *number* is broken down into smaller concepts: addition, subtraction, multiplication, and so on, which are then broken down even further. Mathematics instructors correctly consider the specific examples of concepts to be their "facts" (e.g., $2 + 2 = 4$, pi $= 3.14$).

So what does each of the Structure of Knowledge examples have in common? Though the content differs, each discipline exhibits the same structure—from specific topics and supporting facts to their related concepts, to the transferable, conceptual understandings—the universal generalizations and principles. Each discipline also has a theory level, but education to date hasn't effectively addressed the concepts and generalization levels, so we begin our work there. Note that we work from the bottom up to determine generalizations: from topics and facts to concepts, to generalizations and principles, to theories. We extrapolate concepts and generalizations from the critical factual content to solidly ground our ideas. To understand the different components in the Structure of Knowledge, let's explore the definitions and examples in greater detail. Check your understanding of the differences between topics and concepts, and facts and generalizations, based on the following definitions.

Structure of Knowledge Components

Topics: Organize a set of facts related to specific people, places, situations, or things.
> *Extension:* Topics *do not transfer.* Related to specific examples.
> *Examples:*

- ◆ Ecosystems in the Amazon rain forest
- ◆ The war in Iraq
- ◆ The Pythagorean theorem
- ◆ Picasso's paintings

Facts: Specific examples of people, places, situations, or things.
> *Extension:* Facts *do not transfer.* Locked in time, place, or situation.
> *Examples:*

- ◆ The tropical nature of the Amazon rain forest creates a dense ecosystem.
- ◆ $2 + 2 = 4$, $3 + 1 = 4$

Concepts: Mental constructs that "umbrella" different topical examples and meet these criteria: timeless, universal, abstract (to different degrees), different examples that share common attributes.

Extension: Concepts *do transfer.* A higher level of abstraction than topics because of their generalizability. Concepts come at different levels of generality, abstractness, and complexity.

Examples:

♦ System
♦ Order
♦ Habitat
♦ Value
♦ Linear function

Generalizations: Two or more concepts stated in a relationship that meet these criteria: generally universal application, generally timeless, abstract (to different degrees), supported by different examples (situational). Enduring, essential understandings for a discipline.

Extension: Generalizations must be tested against, and supported by, the facts. May need qualifiers (*often, can, may*) in the sentence if not always true.

Examples:

♦ Organisms adapt to changing environments in order to survive.
♦ Individuals or events can create key turning points in history.
♦ A composite number can be expressed as the combination of prime numbers.
♦ Numbers can be added together in different ways to reach a common sum.
♦ The combined use of subtle and bold colors in a rendering can suggest complexity of emotion.

Principles: Also two or more concepts stated in a relationship, but they are considered the foundational "truths" of a discipline.

Extension: Do not use qualifiers (*often, can, may*) in the sentence. Critical understandings in a discipline (e.g., the *axioms* of mathematics, or the *laws* of science). Like the universal generalizations, principles are referred to as "enduring or essential understandings" or "big ideas" in educational circles.

Examples:

♦ The supply and demand of goods and services affect cost.
♦ In the absence of forces, an object at rest will stay at rest, and an object moving at a constant velocity in a straight line will continue doing so indefinitely.
♦ Any straight line can be extended indefinitely in a straight line.
♦ All right angles are congruent.

Theories: Explanations of the nature or behavior of a specified set of phenomena based on the best evidence available (assumptions, accepted principles, procedures).

Extension: Theories are supported by best evidence rather than absolute facts.

Examples:

♦ The big bang theory of the universe origins
♦ The land bridge theory of early human migration
♦ VESPR theory (valence shell electron-pair repulsion model) in chemistry

Figure 2.3

SOURCE: David Ford Cartoons, davidford@cablespeed.com. Used with permission.

Because the change process can be overwhelming at times, I suggest that educators concentrate their curriculum and instruction redesign efforts on the generalization/principle level—leaving the theory level on idle for now. We can make greater gains with a half-step in change efforts rather than a quantum leap. Teachers will still address theories in their instruction, but we can concentrate our curriculum design efforts on the other levels when introducing the Structure of Knowledge.

A CONCEPT-BASED JOURNEY

I am often asked how I got interested in concepts and the structure of knowledge. Nineteen years ago, while working as a curriculum director in a larger school district south of Seattle, Washington, our Science Committee invited Professor David Cox, from Portland State University, to speak on the topic of concept-based science. His message certainly got my attention! I turned to the teacher next to me—"This is significant. Why haven't I heard more about the importance of concepts for curriculum and instruction?"

Over the next eight years, our curriculum committees pulled out the grade-level concepts framing the factual content for each discipline K–12. But in those days, I was just beginning my own journey of understanding. I did not know how to write the generalizations and principles—nor did I fully understand their importance in teaching and learning. Over the years, my understanding of concept-based curriculum evolved, following a general path of scaffolding insights:

Years 1–5

♦ Concepts allow us to categorize concrete or factual examples.
♦ Concepts have the following attributes: timeless, abstract, universal, different examples with common attributes.
♦ Concepts require a deeper level of understanding than facts.

Years 6–9

♦ Generalizations (universal) are the relationships between two or more concepts and are stated as sentences.
♦ Generalizations have the following attributes: generally timeless, abstract, universal, different situational examples that support the generalization.
♦ Principles are written as generalizations, but do not use qualifying adverbs (*often*, *can*, *may*) in the sentence because they are considered the foundational truths of the discipline (e.g., axioms in mathematics, economic principles, or science laws, such as Newton's or Boyle's laws). There are far more generalizations than principles in a discipline.

Years 10–12

♦ Teaching *inductively* to generalizations and principles, using the fact base as a tool, develops deeper understanding of the factual information and also highlights the conceptual, transferable significance of knowledge.

Years 13–18

♦ The design of concept-based curriculum and instruction is a three-dimensional model because of the prominent role of the conceptual dimension. The three-dimensional model raises the bar for teaching and learning because teachers and students must move beyond the more traditional two-dimensional model of coverage of information and engage the intellect on two levels—factual and conceptual.
♦ The development of intelligence requires a conscious curriculum and instruction design effort to set up a synergistic interplay between the factual and conceptual levels of thinking.

♦ The conceptual mind is the personal intellect. This personal intellect finds relevance, sees patterns and connections, transfers knowledge, and is a key to the motivation for learning.

I tell you all this to reassure those of you who are on the journey that an understanding of the Structure of Knowledge and its applications will take time. This book is intended to provide a shortcut for your journey. Celebrate the small steps, as well as your epiphanies, along the way.

THE PARADIGM SHIFT FOR EDUCATORS

The paradigm shift, to shape the conceptual mind, requires teaching inductively to the concepts, generalizations, and principles using the topics and facts as a supporting tool rather than a final destination. There are two important points to this statement.

1. Teaching inductively means that students are *guided* to understanding concepts, principles, and generalizations. The generalizations and principles are not *generally* taught directly as facts because this robs the student of the opportunity to think things through to deeper levels of understanding. This is why constructivism and inquiry teaching are valued in concept-based teaching and learning models. When students reach adulthood, they will not have someone telling them the big ideas. They will need to analyze information independently to derive a deeper understanding of situations and events. Teachers can help students learn this bridging skill. But prior to instruction, teachers must clearly articulate for themselves the focus concepts and ideas they are guiding students toward. And this is where traditional curriculum documents fail to provide critical support for the teacher's work. Traditional curriculum documents list a plethora of *objectives*—verbs followed by a topic or concept—that only *assume* that teaching will reach conceptual understanding. But we cannot assume teaching for deeper conceptual understanding. Curriculum documents need revision to effectively support teachers with concept-based instruction.

2. Using topics and facts as a supporting tool rather than a final destination will truly raise academic and teaching standards. Students will still learn facts—but the learning will be ultimately focused on deeper conceptual understanding, which gives relevance and purpose to the factual study. Too many teachers still see their job as mainly teaching facts and skills. If you ask a high school history teacher, "Why are you teaching about the American Civil War?" you will likely get a response related to the specific facts, such as, "So my students will understand the different perspectives of the North and South regarding the issue of slavery." A concept-based teacher would answer, "So my students understand the lesson of history that 'Civil war can develop from a clash in perspectives, based on strongly held beliefs and values.'" The teacher would guide students to this understanding by using the American Civil War not as an end point, but as a

tool—a concrete example to develop deeper understanding and to engage the personal intellect of students. Yes—the facts would be taught and tested, but the teacher would also take thinking beyond the facts. Which teacher is developing intellectual character?

In *How People Learn: Brain, Mind, Experience, and School* (2000), John Bransford, Ann Brown, and Rodney Cocking present a powerful and insightful summary of the science of teaching and learning. They explore how novices and experts in any field organize knowledge, and explain how the conceptual brain schema affects one's ability to comprehend and represent problems. "Experts' thinking seems to be organized around big ideas in physics such as Newton's second law and how it would apply, while novices tend to perceive problem solving in physics as memorizing, recalling, and manipulating equations to get answers" (Bransford, Brown, & Cocking, 2000, pp. 37–38). The authors conclude that a strong base of factual knowledge is important for thinking and problem solving (one cannot think about nothing), but experts make knowledge usable by connecting and organizing it around critical concepts that facilitate appropriate transfer to other situations or contexts. For example, if one were to take a position on the national economic benefits of NAFTA (North American Free Trade Alliance) one would need more than the facts related to particular trade relationships, product sales abroad, and foreign purchases. One would need to understand economic and mathematics concepts such as cost/benefit ratio, national trade deficit, and balance of trade, as well as related concepts of economic power tied to political power. Bransford et al. remind us of the obvious—"The fact that experts' knowledge is organized around important ideas or concepts suggests that curricula should also be organized in ways that lead to conceptual understanding" (2000, p. 42).

The paradigm shift to a three-dimensional, concept-based model is not a simple task. It is akin to the first grader who learns what it means to really read when he or she grasps the sound/symbol relationship, the relationship of words to sentences, and that print has meaning. Teachers say, "The reading lightbulb came on for Tommy this week." So it is with understanding the significant relationship of the Structure of Knowledge to curriculum design and instruction. Deep understanding and intellectual development depend on growing points of light—teacher by teacher.

THE TEXAS DEPTH AND COMPLEXITY MODEL

About three years ago, I was shown an interesting model to help make the concept-based paradigm shift in Texas. This model, called the Texas depth and complexity model, was developed by the Texas Education Agency using the insightful work of strong leaders in the Texas education reform movement. Understanding of this model, shown in Figure 2.4, is a required part of the Texas school administrators' recertification process for the state. And now the model is being moved across teacher inservice programs in Texas. This model and explanation could help educators in all states understand the importance of the conceptual level in raising academic achievement for all children.

When the change process starts with current understanding, the likelihood of success is greater. Teachers are all familiar with Bloom's taxonomy and objectives, so it makes sense to begin there.

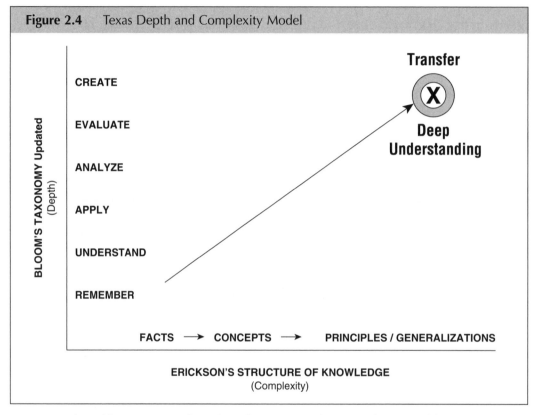

Figure 2.4   Texas Depth and Complexity Model

With the permission of the Texas Education Agency, I have adapted the original model slightly to conform to the updated and revised form of Bloom's original taxonomy, as edited and presented by Lorin Anderson and David Krathwohl (who worked with Bloom on the original taxonomy) in *A Taxonomy for Learning, Teaching, and Assessing: A Revision of Bloom's Taxonomy of Educational Objectives* (2001, p. 310).

Figure 2.5 shows the structural changes from Bloom's original framework to the revision (2001, p. 310).

The depth and complexity model shown in Figure 2.4 illustrates that it is no longer sufficient in education to just rely on Benjamin Bloom's taxonomy because we can take any topic and address it with different levels of verbs, but we are still talking about that specific topic. For example, we can *analyze* and *evaluate* a topic

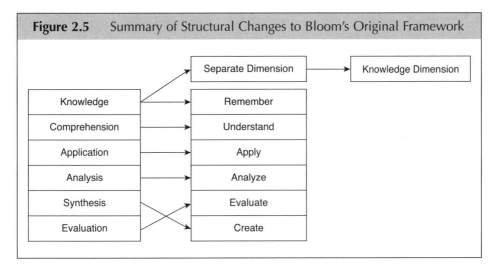

Figure 2.5 Summary of Structural Changes to Bloom's Original Framework

SOURCE: From Lorin W. Anderson, David R. Krathwohl, *A Taxonomy for Learning, Teaching, and Assessing: A Revision of Bloom's Taxonomy of Educational Objectives*. Published by Allyn & Bacon, Boston, MA. © 2001 by Pearson Education. Reprinted by permission of the publisher.

Note: Several important aspects related to the structural changes of Bloom's original frameworks need to be mentioned:

1. The contributors to the book examined more recent frameworks and research on learning and reached a consensus that there are basically four types of knowledge: factual, conceptual, procedural, and metacognitive (Anderson & Krathwohl, 2001, p. 307). Each of these types of knowledge draws on cognitive processes, such as apply, analyze, evaluate, and create.

2. The original framework used noun forms to delineate the six major categories, but the authors of the updated framework determined that it would be more useful to use the verb forms teachers employ in writing objectives and that represent "cognitive processes incorporated with cognitive theory and research" (Anderson & Krathwohl, 2001, p. 307).

3. They also realized that educators relate to the term *understand* rather than *comprehend*, so they chose that descriptor.

4. They interchanged the order of the top two categories, renaming "Synthesis" as "Create" and placing it as the final category beyond "Evaluate."

like "poverty and suffering in the Sudan"—but we are still talking specifically about poverty and suffering in the Sudan. To have deeper, conceptual understanding, we need to draw out the key concepts and guide students inductively to significant, enduring understandings. One understanding for the Sudan topic might be "Cultural groups with limited resources are susceptible to domination and oppression by more powerful groups," or "Displacement of a people can lead to poverty and suffering."

In the depth and complexity model, content objectives using cognitive verbs lead to a synergistic weave with related concepts and generalizations. The ultimate "target" in the depth and complexity model is in the upper right corner, where the deeper factual knowledge intersects with the deeper conceptual understanding. This target for curriculum and instruction is critical for several reasons:

♦ *Deeper understanding of content*—if students do not understand the deeper concepts and principles behind the supporting factual content, their knowledge will only be superficial and fleeting.

♦ *Transfer of knowledge*—when knowledge has been extrapolated from the factual to the conceptual level, it can be transferred through time and across cultures and situations. This not only is an indication of deeper understanding but also allows an individual to see patterns and connections and create new knowledge.

♦ *Development and shaping of the conceptual mind*—the conceptual mind is a beautiful thing. It is the harmonizer of cacophony, the orchestrator of insight, and the Webmaster of design. But traditional curriculum and instruction models fail to give it the prominent billing it deserves.

I would use the Texas depth and complexity model to nudge educators from where they are to understanding the importance of the conceptual level. As soon as they gain this understanding, however, I would drop teaching by objectives and teach inductively to ideas through the use of questions and quality instructional experiences. I would only use the cognitive process verbs in the design of instructional activities or assessments. Teaching to ideas is dynamic teaching and learning; covering objectives runs the risk of being horribly didactic.

Anderson and Krathwohl, in the revision of Bloom's taxonomy, state that there is a difference between the factual and conceptual levels of knowledge:

> By separating Factual knowledge from Conceptual knowledge, we highlight the need for educators to teach for deep understanding of Conceptual knowledge, not just for remembering isolated and small bits of Factual knowledge. Research has shown that many students do not make the important connections between and among the facts they learn in classrooms and the larger system of ideas reflected in an expert's knowledge of a discipline. (2001, p. 42)

There are times when a teacher wants to concentrate on direct instruction of factual knowledge. The goal may be for students to learn, and even memorize, specific content. There are also times when a teacher is giving direct instruction on specific skills. These kinds of direct instruction are certainly supported when the end goals are specific knowledge and skills. This book stresses the need for taking teaching and learning beyond the factual level, however, because it is not occurring enough in the daily work of classrooms.

Conceptual thinking is critical to deeper understanding. The contributors to *A Taxonomy for Learning, Teaching, and Assessing* (2001, p. 70) make a strong point:

> Students understand when they build connections between the "new" knowledge to be gained and their prior knowledge. More specifically, the incoming knowledge is integrated with existing schemas and cognitive frameworks. Since concepts are the building blocks for these schemas and frameworks, conceptual knowledge provides a basis for understanding.

Education needs to increase the percentage of time spent on the factual/conceptual relationships of knowledge. Children with strong conceptual structures in the brain are better able to process the massive amounts of incoming information, and better able to transfer (make use of) knowledge.

Figure 2.6

SOURCE: David Ford Cartoons, davidford@cablespeed.com. Used with permission.

SHAPING CONCEPTUAL UNDERSTANDING GRADE BY GRADE

Concepts represent different levels of generality and complexity. Each discipline has concepts that range from macro to micro. Macroconcepts, such as system, change, and order, are often called "integrating concepts" because they can collapse many different examples. If I understand generally what a *system* is—and how it works, I can transfer that understanding across different types of systems (social, economic, environmental, etc.). These macroconcepts are important, for they provide the broadest categories for structuring knowledge. Each discipline has its own set of macroconcepts to reflect its knowledge base. Some macroconcepts are the same across disciplines. *Change,* for example, is a macroconcept in all disciplines. But there can also be differences in the organizing macroconcepts. (Drama, for example, might use the concepts of character, voice, movement, theme, and design as its broadest, organizing concepts.)

Because macroconcepts have the greatest transferability, many teachers think this is the appropriate target for instruction. So their big ideas are *really* big—such as "Systems are interdependent" or "Change is inevitable." But to make these macro ideas the main target of instruction overlooks the value of microconcepts and their relationships at each grade level.

Macroconcepts provide *breadth* of understanding; but it is the microconcepts that provide *depth* of understanding. Microconcepts reflect the deeper knowledge of the specific discipline. The "experts" in a discipline have the greatest command of the microconcepts and their relationships—and can relate the microconcepts to the broader, organizing concepts of the discipline (see Chart 2.1).

Chart 2.1   Examples of Macro- and Microconcepts

Macroconcepts:	*Microconcepts:*	
Change	microorganism	niche
System	electronegativity	magnitude
Order	slope	linear function
Interdependence	value	intensity
Complexity	oppression	isolationism

Educators who help students develop increasing conceptual depth and understanding by extending their repertoire of discipline-based microconcepts and relationships each year are shaping conceptual minds. My previous book *Stirring the Head, Heart, and Soul* (2001) provides macro- and microconcepts for a variety of subject areas.

Transferable generalizations are statements of conceptual relationship. If we articulate these conceptual understandings through the grades by discipline, we would see a powerful, idea-centered curriculum emerge, supported by factual content.

Chart 2.2 shares examples of enduring understandings (generalizations) through the grades. The concepts in each sentence are italicized. Notice the increasing conceptual sophistication of the generalizations from grade level to grade level. Think about the factual content students would have to know to support their conceptual understanding. Consider the transferability of these ideas through time and across cultures or situations.

Chart 2.2   Enduring, Essential Understandings

	Grade 2	*Grade 4*	*Grade 8*	*Grade 11*
Social Studies	*Community members* cooperate to meet *needs* and *wants.*	People adapt to and alter *environments* to meet *changing needs* and *wants.*	People develop and improve on *tools* and *technologies* to more *efficiently* and *effectively* address their *changing needs* and *wants.*	As *societies* develop *transportation* and *trade networks, social, economic,* and *political interactions* with other *regions* lead to both *cooperative* and *competitive social, economic,* and *political relationships.*
Science	*Living things* interact with their *environment.*	*Organisms* adapt to *changing environments* in order to *survive.*	*Organisms* occupy specific *niches* in a *habitat.*	The *population* of a *species* will grow to fill any available *habitat* to which it can *adapt.*
Mathematics	*Numbers* can be used to *order things or events.*	*Numbers* can have an *inverse relationship.*	*Parts of wholes* can be expressed as *fractions, decimals,* or *percentages.*	*Exponents* and *logarithms* are *inverse operations.*
Visual Arts	*Line* can express *emotion* or *mood.*	*Repetition of lines* can imply *texture* or *pattern.*	*Converging lines* can create the *illusion* of *depth.*	The *movement* of the *artist's* hand determines the *quality* of a *line.*
Language Arts — Writer's Craft	*Authors* choose certain *words* to express *emotions.*	An *author's word choice* can engage or alienate a *reader.*	The *audience* and *purpose* for *writing* determines an *author's writing style.*	*Writing* that has *clarity, precision,* and *depth* reflects the *thinking dispositions* of the *author.*
Theme	*Perspective* shapes *behavior.*	*Characters, real* and *fictional,* who demonstrate *courage* in *difficult situations* can inspire others as they deal with their own *adversity.*	People faced with *social injustice* may choose to *submit* or *revolt.*	*Extreme stress* can lead to *feelings* of *alienation* and *loneliness.*
Structure	*Stories* are organized with a *beginning,* a *middle,* and an *end.*	*Biographies* and *historical fiction* organized by *time frames* guide a *reader* through the *sequence of events.*	*Signal words* identify the *organizational patterns* of *text.*	*Tools* (e.g., *graphic organizers*) that represent *text structure* enhance the *recall* and *understanding* of *text.*

Concepts in Language Arts

In my past work, I only dealt with thematic and writer's craft concepts in language arts, but over the years I developed a nagging feeling that there are some other concepts in this area. My East Coast friend and colleague Dr. Lois Lanning, assistant superintendent in the Pomperaug School District in Connecticut, and I began to have lengthy discussions about concepts in the language arts. Lois has long been an advocate for high literacy standards and has a strong reputation as a language arts consultant. We offer some of our discussions and thinking to this point as a springboard for your own work with language arts concepts.

Lois and I agree that when we are dealing with the specific skills across the strands of language arts (reading, writing, speaking, listening, and viewing), it would be a distraction to worry about big ideas. Big ideas reflect *conceptual understanding.* Reading, writing, speaking, listening, and viewing represent *procedural knowledge,* for the most part.

I questioned Lois to probe the extension of her thinking:

Lois: Within the strands of language arts, there are essential strategies that subsume numerous supporting skills. Knowing how to execute these strategies and skills (procedural knowledge) efficiently and effectively is critical to the development of literacy competence.

Lynn: So how does a learner develop a deep knowledge and conceptual understanding of reading, writing, speaking, listening, and viewing?

Lois: I suggest it is through ongoing, meaningful practice, applying essential language arts strategies and skills to an abundant variety of texts and through the study of the concepts in text. As a learner discovers the rich synergy between the strategic processing of text and the understanding of text concepts, he or she achieves a deep and long-lasting understanding of the text.

[Figure 2.7 illustrates this relationship.]

Lynn: What do you mean by *text,* and is it important to develop a deep understanding of the concepts in text through the grade levels?

Lois: Text is the primary vehicle used to study the language arts. I refer to the term *text* as any medium of communication (e.g., electronic/written text, film, digital, oral, etc.). A rich reservoir of specific concepts is concentrated within text. Different types of text provide many examples for considering transferable concepts. [See Chart 2.3.] To be an expert in language arts, one must fully understand the various macro- and microconcepts found in text. The complex concepts in text are worth teaching directly and through the grade levels because literacy is a long-term developmental process. It takes years to unpack the sophisticated relationships of text concepts.

Lynn: Can you give me an example?

Lois: Here is a reading example: Reading strategies and skills allow initial access to text and enable the reader to make sense of what is being read. A reader is able to go further and be much more critical and reflective about the story if the concept of *character* is understood. A conceptual understanding of character allows the reader to evaluate the character as presented by the author. . . . Deep comprehension involves the personalization or transformation of text at the conceptual level. In other words, readers form their idea of character by filtering the concept through their prior knowledge bank—and then use that personalized conceptual lens to better evaluate and gain a deeper understanding of the character presented by the author. Conceptual depth builds as text is considered from multiple perspectives: the perspective of the reader, viewer, or listener, as well as the perspective of the writer.

Figure 2.7 illustrates Dr. Lanning's ideas related to the synergy between procedural knowledge and conceptual understanding.

Katie Wood Ray (1999), the author of *Wondrous Words: Writers and Writing in the Elementary Classroom*, explains the rationale of teaching text concepts

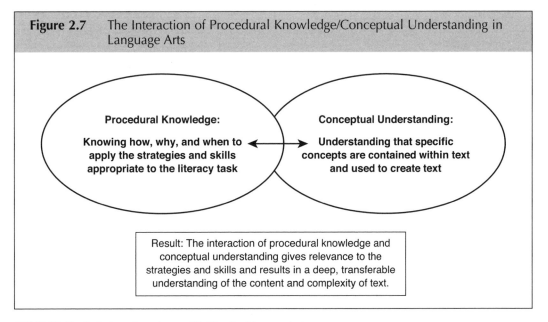

Figure 2.7   The Interaction of Procedural Knowledge/Conceptual Understanding in Language Arts

Procedural Knowledge:

Knowing how, why, and when to apply the strategies and skills appropriate to the literacy task

Conceptual Understanding:

Understanding that specific concepts are contained within text and used to create text

Result: The interaction of procedural knowledge and conceptual understanding gives relevance to the strategies and skills and results in a deep, transferable understanding of the content and complexity of text.

SOURCE: Dr. Lois Lanning, Avon, CT. Used with permission.

when she says that thoughtful readers not only delve into text as readers, but also read text as writers. This is why the concepts of text, such as writer's craft, are important to all the strands of language arts. A deep understanding and appreciation of the complexities of language arts are achieved as procedural knowledge and conceptual understanding of text develop over time.

In Chart 2.3, Dr. Lanning looks at the macro- and microconcepts in text (fiction and nonfiction), which suggest important conceptual understandings.

Chart 2.3 Concepts in Text

Types of Text	Sample Macroconcepts	Sample Microconcepts
FICTION	**ELEMENTS**	**Character:** Protagonist, Antagonist, Dynamic/Static, Hero/Tragic Hero, Foil
		Plot: Causality, Foreshadowing, Suspense, Conflict, Motivation
		Setting: Historical, Future, Cultural Context, Environment
	STRUCTURE/FORM	Cumulative, Interlocking, Circle Story, Classical, Minimalist, Surreal
	GENRE	Mysteries, Folk Tales, Historical Fiction, Short Stories, Poetry, Science Fiction, Comedy, Tragedy, Plays
	THEME	Prejudice and Perspective, Heroes, Loneliness, Fairness
	WRITER'S CRAFT	**Ideas:** Purpose, Originality, Topics
		Organization: Structure, Leads, Transitions, Details, Order, Conclusions, Pattern
		Voice: Tone, Audience, Emotion
		Word Choice: Figurative and Sensory Language, Alliteration, Onomatopoeia, Symbolism
		Sentence Fluency: Rhythm, Cadence, Flow
		Conventions: Mechanics, Punctuation, Presentation, Grammar, Format, Epigrams, Epithets

Types of Text	Sample Macroconcepts	Sample Microconcepts
NONFICTION	**ELEMENTS**	**Subject/Character, Issue or Exigency (event demanding a response):** Main Idea, Supporting Details, Events
		Audience: Targeted, General Public
		Purpose: Exposure, Explanation, Definition, Persuasion, Analysis/Synthesis, Argument, Propaganda, Description, Motivation
	STRUCTURE/FORM	Cause/Effect, Problem/Solution, Exposition, Temporal, Compare/Contrast
	GENRE	Biography/Autobiography, Technical, Essay, Satire, Historical, Persuasive, Poetry
	THEME	Social Reform, Conflict/Cooperation, Courage, Power/Influence
	WRITER'S CRAFT (see macroconcepts under Writer's Craft in the Fiction section of this chart)	(See microconcepts under Writer's Craft in the Fiction section of this chart)

SOURCE: Dr. Lois Lanning, Avon, CT. Used with permission.

SUMMARY

When teachers know how knowledge is structured, it informs their teaching. Educators should not be graduating from teacher training institutions without this information. Yet the majority of educators have not even been trained on the differences between a topic and a concept, and a fact and a generalization. They know intuitively, but need the discussion with their subject area content.

This chapter discusses the relationship between the Structure of Knowledge and the curriculum and instruction that plays out each day in classrooms. Teachers are concerned when they realize that so many of our curriculum textbooks and materials cover the lowest level of topics and facts, and *assume* that students will understand the deeper concepts and principles.

Teachers need practice in extrapolating the key concepts, generalizations, and principles from the topics and facts they teach. This is hard work because teachers have not been previously asked to generalize the deeper understandings from what they teach. Yet, if we have any hope of developing the intelligence of our students to sophisticated levels, curriculum and instruction must shift the paradigm from covering objectives to using the factual content as a tool to develop deeper understanding of underlying concepts, principles, and generalizations.

This chapter shares a model from Texas (depth and complexity model) that is helping teachers and administrators realize the importance of the conceptual level of understanding. This model is a good first step in nudging us out of the box.

Across disciplines, we are working to identify conceptual structures—the concepts and generalizations/principles that frame the timeless nature of knowledge. We realize that mathematics is a language of conceptual relationships that must be delineated in word as well as number sentences. And we look at language arts and consider how best to define the conceptual structure that brings out the depth of the discipline.

The changes that are needed to improve intellectual development, as well as academic performance, require curriculum rewrites—not only at the school district level, but also at the state level. Academic standards are incoherent in their cross-disciplinary design. Chapter 3 addresses the concerns with academic standards as they relate to concept-based curriculum and instruction.

EXTENDING THOUGHT

1. How would you explain the different levels in the Structure of Knowledge to a new teacher in your building?

2. Why is an understanding of the Structure of Knowledge critical to quality curriculum design and instruction?

3. What is the difference between two-dimensional and three-dimensional curriculum? . . . instruction? How close are you to a three-dimensional model in your teaching? What are your "next steps" on the journey?

4. What is the main point of the Texas depth and complexity model?

5. What is the difference, and relationship, between macro- and microconcepts? Why do we want to expand a student's repertoire of microconcepts and related generalizations through the grades in addition to the macroconcepts?

6. How do macroconcepts provide breadth of knowledge? How do microconcepts provide depth of knowledge?

7. What is your reaction to the discussion of language arts concepts related to text in this chapter?

Meeting Academic Standards With Integrity

3

WHAT ACADEMIC STANDARDS ARE

National and state academic standards in the United States were developed to identify clearly what students are to know and be able to do in the different disciplines of knowledge. They arose out of concern in the 1980s for the low test scores when the United States was compared to other industrialized nations, out of concerns from employers who decried the lack of knowledge and skills among entry-level workers, and from national research studies with doomsday predictions if the United States did not upgrade the educational program for students.

At the national level, discipline-based committees developed documents framing what they considered to be the most critical knowledge and skills for their subject area. Each committee also determined the design format for these documents.

Following the national lead, state-level committees drafted what they considered to be the most critical knowledge and skills for their students. The committees were again discipline based, and leaned heavily on the national documents to frame their work.

Finally, discipline-based committees at the school district level worked to develop curricular frameworks that aligned to the state-level standards.

So, theoretically, teachers should have a very clear understanding of what they must teach their students. And, as an educational consultant who has worked with schools around the country pre- and poststandards era, I certainly think the standards movement has raised expectations for both teachers and students. It has also brought more structure and vertical articulation to the prekindergarten through high school curriculum. But we still have revision work to do in the design of academic standards, the training of teachers, and problems associated with resources (specifically, time and money) and accountability (teachers, parents, administrators, and government).

Teachers have a challenging job. They are expected to meet the heavy mandates of academic standards in spite of tremendous diversity in learning needs and the limits of time. The intent of standards is to improve student performance—a laudable goal. But we let our teachers and students down when we crack the whip of expectations without actively addressing shortfalls in curriculum design and teacher training.

WHAT ACADEMIC STANDARDS ARE NOT

Academic standards are not a curriculum; they are a framework for designing curriculum. A curriculum is a coherent, teacher-friendly document that *reflects* the intent of the academic standards. When teachers mistakenly think that state academic standards are a curriculum, they may start checking off benchmarks one by one, which can lead to pellet-gun teaching. A high school history teacher said to me proudly, "I am checking off every benchmark in the state standard*s cur-riculum* to make certain I do everything it says." I saw the picture in my mind:

- ◆ Explain the importance of the following dates in U.S. History: 1607, 1776, 1803 . . .
- ◆ Analyze causes of the American Revolution
- ◆ Explain the issues surrounding events of the American Revolution . . .
- ◆ Analyze the issues of the Philadelphia Convention of 1787 . . .
- ◆ Describe major problems faced by leaders of the New Republic . . .
- ◆ Explain the impact of the election of Andrew Jackson, including the origins of the modern Democratic Party . . . and so on—*through more than 100 benchmarks!*

My heart sank. I knew that this teacher's students were racing over complex material trying to memorize and regurgitate information to pass the tests.

Academic standards are not a quick fix or a sure panacea to the problems in education. If they were, we would have seen even greater improvements in the educational achievement of our students by this time. Though there have been some improvements, the overall reports are still discouraging. The most recent PISA (Programme for International Student Assessment) test results comparing the reading and math skills of 15-year-olds in a large group of industrialized nations and a smaller group of developing countries ranked the United States 24th out of 29 nations in math literacy. Problem-solving abilities came in with the same ranking (Programme for International Student Assessment, 2003).

I am convinced that one major reason academic achievement has not yet met our expectations is that the national, state, and, consequently, district standards documents lack cross-disciplinary *coherence* and intellectual depth in their designs. In many states, we need less content coverage and greater conceptual depth. If you examine the performance indicators across academic standards in science, social studies, and mathematics, you will find that science is generally concept based, social studies is fact based, and mathematics is skill based. Figure 3.2 illustrates this point using the typical design models for each subject area. Can you see the conceptual and factual designs, respectively, in the science and social studies examples? What is the effect of these two designs on classroom instruction?

Figure 3.1

SOURCE: David Ford Cartoons, davidford@cablespeed.com. Used with permission.

Figure 3.2 Sample Performance Indicators

Science	Social Studies	Mathematics
The student *understands* that . . . adaptations may increase the survival of members of a species.	The student *knows* . . . the social, economic, and political challenges that were confronted by the North and the South during the American Civil War.	The student *uses* . . . place value to represent whole numbers and decimals.

Now look at the mathematics example. Notice that it tells what students will *do*, rather than what they will *understand*. Conceptual understanding is assumed. Granted, students must be able to do the skills. But students who perform skills perfunctorily do not necessarily have an understanding of the underlying mathematical concepts. Writing mathematics generalizations to reflect the deeper understandings of skills is difficult work for teachers who have not been trained to articulate these ideas. Mathematics is a language of conceptual relationships. Yet we seldom see those relationships written in sentence form in curriculum documents—nor are teachers expected to help students verbalize those relationships.

Certainly we need the developmental articulation of mathematics skills through the grades; but we also need a stated set of mathematical relationships (generalizations) to give relevance to the skills.

I recently had the pleasure of working with teachers in the Mathematics and Science Academy at Ocean Lakes High School in Virginia Beach, Virginia. Let's look at samples of the enduring understandings they wrote for one unit within their various courses.

Magnet Geometry: Unit Title—Similarity (Josephine Letts)

▶ A change in one dimension of similar objects results in changes in area and volume in predictable ratios.

▶ A constant ratio exists between lengths of corresponding parts of similar figures.

▶ Similar figures are dilations of each other or transformational images of each other.

▶ Specific angle/side formulas identify similar triangles that are not dependent on the position of the triangle.

▶ Proportional relationships contained in similar triangles enable calculation of measurements that are not otherwise accessible.

▶ Scale factor represents the constant ratio that is the essential component for creating models and scale drawings.

Magnet Advanced Algebra: Unit Title—Trigonometry (Lisa Anderson, Susan John, and Karel Wetzel)

▶ Every degree measure has an equivalent radian measure based on the circumference of a circle.

▶ The value of the trigonometric functions of an angle is determined from the ratios of the lengths of the sides of a right triangle.

▶ Rotation determines quadrant, which leads to the sign of the value of the trigonometric functions.

▶ Every trigonometric function of any angle can be evaluated by using the cosine and sine of the reference angle.

Magnet Precalculus I: Unit Title—Sequences and Series (Lori Burwell and Judy Darden)

▶ A factorial represents a special kind of product often used to define the pattern of a sequence or series.

▶ Sigma notation indicates the operation of summation.

▶ Formulas exist to find the terms or the sum of certain arithmetic or geometric sequences and series.

▶ An interdependent relationship exists between the order of terms and the pattern of a sequence or series.

▶ A series represents a function whose domain is a subset of the positive integers.

▶ Testing for convergence or divergence provides insight into the nature of a series.

Multivariable Calculus: Unit Title—Vectors in Space (Carolyn Doetsch and Venesa Reyes)

▶ A coordinate system in 3-D requires a third variable to represent the additional dimension.

▶ Planes, spheres, quadric surfaces, cylindrical surfaces, and surfaces of revolution model physical behavior.

▶ Vector-valued functions trace the physical path of an object.

▶ The derivative and integral represent position, velocity, or acceleration of an object moving along a path.

▶ Arc length represents the distance that an object travels along a path.

▶ The magnitude of the curvature correlates to the speed and sharpness of the curve.

▶ Limits and continuity of vector-valued functions must exist to determine the acceleration of an object along a path.

▶ Cross-sections indicate behavior of the function in two of the three dimensions.

Magnet Computer Architecture: Unit Title—Number Systems (Diana Hirschi)

Positional Numbering Systems

▶ A numeric value is represented through increasing powers of a radix (base).

Binary Representations

▶ The binary number system lies at the heart of virtually every electronic device that relies on digital controls.

Conversions of Unsigned Numbers

▶ Knowing the base of a number system enables one to convert from one number system to another.

Words and Numbers

▶ The size of a word limits the magnitude of the numbers that can be represented, and overflow occurs when the limit is reached.

▶ Signed and unsigned numbers have different representations.

▶ The computer models an infinite real number system with a finite system of integers, leading to floating point errors.

The enduring understandings from the Mathematics and Science Academy at Ocean Lakes High School are strong conceptual understandings that give focus for teaching their units. Mathematics teachers at all grade levels and in all courses need to write out these understandings to accompany their skills.

It would be so easy to bring design coherence across the disciplinary standards provided by each state. If we follow the lead of science in Figure 3.2 and turn the social studies and mathematics examples into conceptual understandings, how might they be written?

♦ Science: The student *understands that* adaptations may increase the survival of members of a species.

♦ Social Studies: The student understands that_____

_____

♦ Mathematics: The student understands that_____

_____

Did you come up with something like this?

♦ Social Studies: The student *understands that* nations engaged in civil war face social, economic, and political challenges that can reshape a culture over time.
♦ Mathematics: The student *understands that* place value can be used to represent whole numbers and decimals.

Notice that the lead-in phrase, "understands that," sets up the structure for the generalization sentence—two or more concepts stated in a relationship.

IDEAS THROUGH THE GRADES

Curriculum documents need to be revised from objective driven to idea centered if we want to develop the intellect and shape the critical and creative thinking of conceptual minds. I know this statement may seem heretical. But let's consider the evidence and logic. Humans tend to be comfortable with established patterns of behavior. And we were all educated under a system called "teaching to objectives." Benjamin Bloom raised our expectations of students by designating specific verbs for different levels of cognitive work—for example, the lower cognitive level of *knowledge* and the higher cognitive level of *synthesis.* And this was a great contribution to education. But I think that today, we are stuck in a perfunctory, verb-slapping design process that fails to ensure the transfer of knowledge and deeper, conceptual understanding.

The great thinkers in history—Plato, Aristotle, Einstein, and so on—did not develop their minds or reach deep understanding by doing verbs with topics. They thought about ideas, issues, and problems. They hypothesized, examined evidence, looked for patterns and connections between facts and the related concepts and principles, and raised questions to challenge their findings. They were, in essence, idea-centered constructivists.

Chart 3.1 lists enduring understandings (generalizations) that would be developmentally appropriate for the maturity levels and content in several grade levels. Notice that the understandings are clearly stated. (Thank you to my friends and colleagues, Patrick Leighton and Jim Jennings, who gave their wise input to the science and mathematics understandings.) Teachers should be able to read an enduring understanding for their grade level and know exactly how it would relate to the factual content they are required to teach.

There is another reason why we need to write statements of conceptual understanding through the grade levels. *Notice all the italicized concepts at each grade level in Chart 3.1. Now imagine if teachers had three to five instructional units per grade level in a subject area, with eight to ten conceptual understandings for each of those units. The depth and breadth of developing conceptual understanding would be powerfully apparent.*

Chart 3.1   Sample Enduring Understandings

Grade 2	*Grade 6*	*High School*
Social Studies	**Social Studies**	**Social Studies**
Culture ♦ *A community* can be a *neighborhood* or many *neighborhoods* that share *public services* such as schools, law enforcement, and hospitals. ♦ *People* in a *community* cooperate to solve *problems* that affect their *daily lives.* **Economics** ♦ *People* purchase *goods* and *services* to meet their *wants* and *needs.* ♦ *People* make *choices* because they cannot have everything they *want.* **Geography** ♦ *Communities* use *natural resources* to meet *basic needs.* ♦ Citizens care for their *environment* to protect the *natural resources.*	**Culture** ♦ *Cultures* are described by *common elements* that relate to their *basic needs* (food, clothing, shelter, religion, family, etc.). ♦ *Cultures* address *human needs* and *concerns* in *similar* and *different ways.* **Economics** ♦ A *country* with *scarce natural resources* will *trade* to obtain *products* that are locally unavailable. **Geography** ♦ *Geographical expansion* for *political* or *economic reasons* may lead to *exploitation* of *native inhabitants.* **History** ♦ Advances in *communications technology* can facilitate the *dissemination of ideas* and *political thought* and revolutionize *cultural worldviews.*	**Culture/Economics** ♦ As *societies* develop *transportation* and *trade networks, social, economic,* and *political interactions* with other *regions* lead to both *cooperative* and *competitive social, economic,* and *political relationships.* **Economics** ♦ *Specialization* and *division of labor* can increase *worker productivity.* ♦ Greater *specialization* leads to greater *interdependence* among *consumers* and *producers.* **Geography/Government** ♦ *Geographical* and *political unification* alter the *social* and *economic structures* of *nations.*

(Continued)

Chart 3.1 (Continued)

Grade 2	Grade 6	High School
Social Studies	**Social Studies**	**Social Studies**
History ◆ *Communities* can *grow* and *change* over *time*. ◆ *Citizens work together* to build a *community*. **Government** ◆ *Communities* have *leaders* with specific *roles*. ◆ *Laws* and *rules* help protect *community members*. ◆ *Citizens* in a *community* have *responsibilities* and *rights*.	**Government/Economics** ◆ To manage the *national economy, government* regulates *business* and *trade* through *monetary policy, tariffs*, and *taxes*.	**Government** ◆ *Nations* use *diplomacy, political* or *economic sanctions*, or *war* to resolve *international conflicts* that affect the *national welfare*. **History** ◆ *Fear* and *distrust* between *nations* can impede *social, political,* and *economic relationships*, making it difficult to secure and enforce *international treaties* and *agreements*.
Science	**Science**	**Science**
Physical Science ◆ *Changes* in *heat* can cause *changes* such as *melting* or *evaporation*. **Life Science** ◆ *Living things* have *external characteristics* that allow them to meet their *basic needs*. ◆ *Plants* and *animals* have *parts* that perform different *functions*. **Earth Science** ◆ The *environment* contains *resources*, such as rocks, soil, water, and gases in the atmosphere, which are useful to people.	**Physical Science** ◆ *Changes* in *thermal energy* always accompany *changes* in *states of matter*, even if the *temperature* does not *change*. ◆ *Substances* can be identified by their chemical and *physical properties*, but their *identities* are dictated by their *composition*. **Life Science** ◆ All *organisms* are composed of *cells* that carry out *functions* to sustain life. ◆ Some *traits* of *species* can change over several *generations* through *natural selection, sexual selection*, or *selective breeding*.	**Chemistry** ◆ *Thermal energy* changes the *state of matter* by influencing the *pattern* of *molecular motion*. ◆ *Physical change* can occur in a *substance* without altering its *identity*, while a *chemical change* implies a *change* in *identity*. ◆ The *concentration* of a *solution* is determined by the *ratio* of *dissolved particles* compared to the *particles* they are dissolved in. ◆ The *energy* of a *reaction* relates to the *gain* or *loss* of *heat* to the *environment*. During any *chemical reaction, heat* is either gained from or lost to its *environment*.

Grade 2	Grade 6	High School
Science	**Science**	**Science**
	Earth Science ♦ *Natural processes*, such as *erosion, earthquakes,* and *volcanoes,* create changes in *landforms.*	**Biology** ♦ *Cells* have *specialized parts* that perform certain *functions,* such as *homeostasis, energy production, transportation* of *molecules, exclusion* and s*election* of *molecules,* disposal of *wastes,* function of *cellular parts,* and synthesis of new *molecules.*
Mathematics	**Mathematics**	**Mathematics**
Number ♦ *Numbers* can show *order* and establish *sequence.* **Patterns** ♦ *Geometric figures* can be arranged to form *repeating patterns.* **Measurement** ♦ *Measurement* can provide a precise description of *properties* such as *distance, volume, mass, temperature,* etc.	**Number** ♦ *Rational numbers,* including *whole numbers, fractions,* and *decimals,* can be expressed in *equivalent forms* of *standard notation* or *scientific notation.* **Patterns** ♦ *Geometric patterns* can be formed by connecting *lines* with *repeated lengths, spacings,* and/or *angles.* **Measurement** ♦ *Estimation* approximates *actual values* of some *measurable property* of an *object, substance,* or *wave.*	**Number** ♦ *Cartesian coordinates* represent the relationship of two *numerical values* linked to the *units of measurement* of each coordinate's *variable.* **Patterns** ♦ In either a *regular* or *nonregular tessellation,* the *sum* of the interior angles of the *shapes* at any *vertex* must equal 360 degrees. **Measurement** ♦ Any *distance (length, width, height, depth, thickness,* or *radius)* is a *one-dimensional measurement* of a *line's magnitude* whether *straight* or *curved.*

The visual arts teachers in Meridian School District No. 2, in Meridian, Idaho, created a flow chart of developing enduring understandings for the elements and principles of visual arts. Figure 3.3 provides an excerpt of these developing ideas for the principle of *movement* and the element of *shape.*

Figure 3.3 Visual Arts Framework Excerpt

Visual Arts: Principles of Design		Concept: Movement	
Enduring Understanding	*Enduring Understanding*		*Enduring Understanding*
Movement can be created using any one or a combination of the elements of art.	Movement is used by artists to guide the viewer's eye through a composition.		Movement may create a variety of feelings.

Guiding Concepts (subgeneralizations)

Movement is achieved through the placement of the elements (listed in next column) so the eye follows a certain path.	The elements of art are line, shape, form, value, color, texture, and space.	Movement helps make certain that the main parts of the artwork are noted.	Creating movement through organic shapes and curved lines can create a calm feeling.	Creating movement through the use of geometric shapes and straight lines may create a feeling of action and energy.	Spacing of the elements may create different moods. Open = lonely, isolated, calm. Tightly compressed = tension, pressure, dissonance.

Lower level → → → → → → → → →   Upper level → → → → → → → → → → →

Guiding Questions
1. **Criticism:** How does the artist move your eye through this artwork?
2. **Aesthetics:** What mood or message is conveyed through movement in this work of art?
3. **History:** Compare the use of movement used by two artists from two different periods in history.

Visual Arts: Elements of Art		Concept: Shape	

Enduring Understanding	*Enduring Understanding*	*Enduring Understanding*
Organic shapes differ from geometric shapes.	Shapes can be used together to create a successful composition.	Shapes and forms are closely linked.

Guiding Concepts

Geometric shapes are precise and man-made.	Organic shapes are often found in nature and are free formed and irregular.	Most objects are a combination of geometric and organic shapes.	Overlapping and repeating shapes can create pattern, harmony, and depth in a design.	Shapes can be used to direct the viewer's eye through the composition.	A form is a shape with three dimensions, having mass and volume.	Artists create the illusion of 3-D form by shading an object with a full range of values.	The light source determines the placement of values.

Lower level → → → → → → → → **Upper level** → → → → → → → → → →

Guiding Questions

1. **Criticism:** Is this piece of artwork dominated by organic or geometric shapes?

2. **Aesthetics:** How does shape influence the meaning of this artwork?

3. **History:** How did Cubist artists use shape in their compositions?

SOURCE: Used with permission of Meridian Joint School District, Meridian, Idaho.

Education today values and promotes many brain-based strategies such as the use of essential questions, constructivism, multiple intelligences, differentiation, and inquiry, yet we keep turning out academic standards, curriculum documents, and textbooks that list the same old objectives to cover (a confusing mix of verb-driven, factual, conceptual, and skill-based statements), rather than a powerful set of ideas to understand and transfer, which are supported by factual information.

It is time to use Benjamin Bloom's verbs where they can be most helpful—in the design of learning experiences and assessments. That is where we want students to analyze, synthesize, evaluate, and create.

I believe the verbs are misplaced in academic frameworks for content standards and performance indicators at the state and district levels. What we need at the state and district levels are documents that provide teachers with three clear categories of information:

What we want students to know (*topical, factual knowledge*)

Example:
Students will *know* . . .

- ◆ the life cycle stages of the butterfly.
- ◆ the key historical figures in the development of (state).

What we want students to understand (the conceptual *transferable understandings* of the discipline)

Example:
Students will *understand that* . . .

- ◆ life cycles ensure the continuation of a species.
- ◆ leaders and events can shape the social, economic, and political directions of a nation.

What we want students to be able to do (the specific *processes and skills* of the discipline)

Example:
The students will *be able to* . . .

- ◆ create models and diagrams that represent natural objects or events.
- ◆ use primary and secondary source documents to analyze a key event in history, and form a generalization (a transferable lesson of history) supported by factual evidence.

The *know* and *understand* categories need statements—without verb lead-ins. But the content standards in most curriculum documents are a confusing mix of factual and conceptual expectations. The skill standards *do* need the verb lead-in, however—"Evaluate text to determine main ideas . . ."

Skills Versus Activities

I have noticed a common misunderstanding among teachers regarding skill standards. When asked to write the skills that they will be bringing into their science or social studies units, they often write statements like the following:

♦ Describe the relationships in a desert food chain using specific examples.
♦ Analyze the events leading up to World War II.

These are content objectives or instructional activities, not skill objectives. Teachers become confused because they see the skill word (*describe*, *analyze*) at the beginning of the sentence. But the focus is actually on the content knowledge in these examples. We need to alert teachers that state standards documents almost always locate the skill standards under one or two sections in both science and social studies. In science, the particular standards that delineate the skills are often referred to as "Inquiry Skills"; in social studies, the skill standards are usually referred to as "Historical Thinking Skills," or "Social Studies Skills." The geography strand also includes some skill indicators along with the content standards. Teachers will want to look beyond the broader skill standard to the specific performance indicators (bullets) to see the specific expectations. Unfortunately, some state skill standards are so weak that teachers have to "beef them up" at the local level. Here are some tips to help teachers understand *skills:*

♦ Skills *transfer*. (Analyze primary and secondary source documents to compare historical perspective.)
♦ When you attach a skill to a particular topic, you have created a *content objective* or an *instructional activity*. (*Analyze* primary and secondary source documents *on the American Civil War* to compare the perspectives of the North and the South.)

CONTEXTUALIZING STANDARDS INTO CLASSROOM CURRICULA

So how would concept-based, three-dimensional history teachers address the know, understand and able to do expectations from academic standards? They would design instructional units for the different historical periods, use a conceptual lens to focus and invite the students to bring their own minds to the study, and contextualize the performance indicators appropriately into the unit study. They would not piecemeal knowledge and understanding. They would design the units holistically and coherently so that students were learning the story *and the lessons* of history, with supporting details. But perhaps most important, they would not simply "check off" the indicators in the standards. Because the performance indicators are currently written as objectives—rather than statements of knowledge or understanding—teachers would ask themselves the questions, "*Why* do this indicator? Is there a lesson of history here for students to understand?" A simple technique would be to add the phrase, "in order to understand that . . ." after key indicators, finishing the phrase with a transferable generalization reflective of the content they teach. They would bring these understandings into their classroom units and use the factual content as support for developing the ideas.

Let's see how Ms. Dale—a concept-based, middle school American history teacher—plans her unit on the American Revolution (see Figure 3.4) and contextualizes the related indicators from the standards. Ms. Dale will write 8–12 generalizations (enduring, essential understandings aligned to the academic standards) for *each* of the five to eight units of instruction she plans for the year. Her goal will be to guide the students to these understandings as she has them work with the factual content. She will teach to—and beyond—the facts. She is a brain-based teacher. She knows that she must create a synergy between the conceptual and factual levels of thinking if her students are to retain the factual content, gain deeper conceptual understanding, and also develop their minds.

You may be wondering why Ms. Dale would be teaching to 8–12 generalizations per unit of instruction. The reason is that there are five strands in social studies standards (history, geography, economics, government, and culture), each with their own concepts and generalizations. We need to address the developing conceptual ideas for all the social studies strands through the grade levels.

Figure 3.4   American History Unit Excerpt

Unit Title: The American Revolution

Conceptual Lens: Freedom/Revolution

Enduring, Essential Understandings:

History (Standards: _____)

- *Significant events* and/or *individual leaders* or *groups* can create *turning points* in the path of *history.*

Economics (Standards: _____)

- *Nations* establish *colonies* to further their *economic* and *political interests.*

Government/Culture (Standards: _____)

- As *countries* under *foreign rule* develop local *social* and *political structures* that reinforce changing *beliefs* and *values,* they may challenge the *inherited rule* of a *mother country.*
- *Political revolutions* are fought to gain *freedoms* from, or *changes* in, *the controlling government* and its *policies.*
- *Nations* may form *alliances* to further *political* and/or *economic self-interests.*

Economics (Standards_____)

- *War* can stimulate, depress, or decimate the *economy* of a *region* or *nation*.

For her unit planning, Ms. Dale will also list the critical, factual content, defined by the academic standards that students must know:

Critical Content (Know examples):

- The reasons for the settlement of the colonies

- The causes of the American Revolution

- The key figures and their roles in the American Revolution

She will also decide on the key skills (what students will be able to do) that will be taught or reinforced in this unit. She will draw these skills from those listed in the state standards.

Key Skills (examples):

- Analyze primary and secondary source documents

- Find locations and trace routes on maps

- Create graphs and charts to display historical data

Once Ms. Dale is clear on what she wants students to know, understand, and be able to do, she is ready to design her assessments and learning activities.

Teachers like Ms. Dale will design quality learning experiences and assessments that align to what she wants her students to know, understand, and be able to do. She would fall into the "Expert Teacher" category (Figure 3.5) if we were to characterize her approach to standards:

Figure 3.5   Rubric: Teaching to Standards

Novice—The standards *are* the curriculum. Teachers *cover* the standards, checking each one off as they go piecemeal through a flurry of skill-driven photocopies, teach and test through a pile of unrelated topics, and try to make sense of a little of this and a little of that.

Practitioner—The standards provide a *set of expectations* for what students must know and be able to do. Teachers *reflect* on the quality and intent of the standards and determine how to efficiently integrate the standards into their classroom curriculum by *contextualizing*— fitting the standards into more holistic units or programs for instruction. They teach to the understanding of individual concepts as they work with content, and they conscientiously teach to skills. They post guiding questions (rather than standards) in their classrooms to engage the intellect and interest of students. The guiding questions relate to what students must *know* and *understand*. They differentiate curriculum, instruction, and the learning environment to meet the diverse needs of learners.

(Continued)

Figure 3.5 (Continued)

Expert—The standards provide a set of expectations for what students must know (factual knowledge), understand (conceptual knowledge), and be able to do (skills and processes). Teachers *analyze* the standards and clearly articulate the *know, understand*, and able to *do* components. This often requires that they infer and write the conceptual understandings when standards are fuzzy. They *contextualize* the *know, understand,* and be able to *do* components into coherent, integrated instructional units, and improve on the expectations of standards at the unit level. They teach inductively to conceptual ideas and strive for deep understanding. They use factual content as a tool to exemplify the deeper meaning of concepts, principles, and generalizations. They understand how knowledge is structured and engage the intellect on different levels and in diverse ways through guiding questions and learning experiences. They strive to deepen their own understanding of the discipline(s) they teach. They engage students in disciplinary ways of knowing and doing. They value constructivism within a structure and differentiation to maximize learning success for all students. They exemplify the art as well as the science of teaching.

SOURCE: *Integrated Curriculum: A Chapter of the Curriculum Handbook*, by H. Lynn Erickson (2003). Association for Supervision and Curriculum Development, Alexandria, VA. Reprinted by permission. The Association for Supervision and Curriculum Development is a worldwide community of educators advocating sound policies and sharing best practices to achieve the success of each learner. To learn more, visit ASCD at www.ascd.org.

All teachers, including Ms. Dale, can benefit from the work of Grant Wiggins and Jay McTighe, colleagues that I hold in high regard for their continuing contributions to teaching for deep understanding and assessment. They recently published an expanded and updated edition of their *Understanding by Design* workbook (Wiggins & McTighe, 2005). Chart 3.2 shares their helpful criteria for describing student performances related to six "facets" of understanding (2005, p. 177). These performances draw upon factual content and skills but demonstrate the deeper enduring understandings of a discipline.

BRINGING DISTRICT-LEVEL COHERENCE TO STANDARDS

Because state academic standards lack cross-disciplinary design coherence, local school districts can rectify the problem in their local standards design work. Because of our traditional focus on covering objectives, most teachers are only tangentially aware of the discipline-based concepts for their grade level and subject areas. And because we have not written out the generalizations—the conceptual relationships—that we expect students to understand at each grade level, we have a fuzzy structure for developing minds. So how can we correct this problem? Two things have to occur in curriculum design at the local level:

Chart 3.2   Facet-Related Criteria

Facet 1 Explanation	Facet 2 Interpretation	Facet 3 Application	Facet 4 Perspective	Facet 5 Empathy	Facet 6 Self-Knowledge
◆ accurate	◆ meaningful	◆ effective	◆ credible	◆ sensitive	◆ self-aware
◆ coherent	◆ insightful	◆ efficient	◆ revealing	◆ open	◆ metacognitive
◆ justified	◆ significant	◆ fluent	◆ insightful	◆ receptive	◆ self-adjusting
◆ systematic	◆ illustrative	◆ adaptive	◆ plausible	◆ perceptive	◆ reflective
◆ predictive	◆ illuminating	◆ graceful	◆ unusual	◆ tactful	◆ wise

SOURCE: Grant Wiggins and Jay McTighe, *Understanding by Design,* Expanded 2nd Edition. © 2005 Alexandria, VA: Association for Supervision and Curriculum Development. Reprinted by permission. The Association for Supervision and Curriculum Development is a worldwide community of educators advocating sound policies and sharing best practices to achieve the success of each learner. To learn more, visit ASCD at www.ascd.org.

◆ *Curriculum committees need to identify the macro- and microconcepts to be taught at each grade level, kindergarten (or preschool) through Grade 12.* This needs to be done for each content area separately. The availability of time and funding will determine how long it takes to complete the job.

◆ *Subject area curriculum committees need to write the generalizations and principles (transferable, conceptual understandings) that reflect the deeper understandings beyond, but related to, the factual knowledge.* These generalizations, when displayed through the grade levels, should show increasing conceptual depth and knowledge. The generalizations should have a few of the macro-level ideas, but the majority of generalizations will reflect the more specific concepts/relationships of the discipline. Macroconcepts provide disciplinary breadth; microconcepts provide disciplinary depth.

Curriculum Leadership

If you are a curriculum leader, you might be wondering how to go about developing concept-based curricula aligned to state academic standards, so here are two different approaches for you to consider. (I favor the first approach for bringing out well-stated generalizations that reflect the deeper intent of state academic standards and the content knowledge of a discipline.)

1. Unit Development Approach

The unit development approach *contextualizes* state academic standards into the school district's core curriculum. This method shows teachers how to address the standards using their content, and clarifies the link between what students must know, understand, and be able to do.

♦ Provide instruction on concept-based curriculum and the Structure of Knowledge for the district curriculum committee. (The goal here is to help the committee understand the difference between topics, concepts, and generalizations/principles, and to internalize the idea of teaching to the conceptual level—concepts and generalizations—using topics and facts as tools for developing deeper understanding.)

♦ Arm the committee with the subject area academic standards from the state, a set of committee-approved unit design steps, and a unit planner.

♦ Using state academic standards and three different colors of markers, have the committee identify key topics (specific, nontransferable) in one color, concepts (transferable, one or two words) in another color, and the skills (transferable abilities) in the last color. Be aware that the skills are usually found in one or two sections in standards documents. Science usually calls the skills area "Inquiry Skills;" social studies may refer to this section as "Historical Thinking" or "Social Studies Skills," and also has skills embedded in the geography section of the standards. Mathematics and language arts are almost all listed as "Skills."

♦ Have each grade level write the major topics for the subject area under development (social studies, science, mathematics, etc.) for the year. These topics will be the focus for designing instructional units.

Rule of thumb:

♦ Elementary grade levels will have three to four units in social studies and three to four units in science for a year. Grades 4–6 might have five units in social studies because of the heavier content load.
♦ Secondary courses will have five to eight instructional units for a year. (If there are more than eight units for a year, teachers will be forced to skim, slide, and crash and burn throughout the year.)

♦ Committee members should bring text and other materials to support the unit development. Remind them that the textbook is a resource, not the curriculum.

♦ In the unit design process, committee members will identify clearly what students must know factually, understand conceptually, and be able to do.

A set of steps for unit design is included in Chapter 4, and a sample unit and lesson planner format for laying out the steps is provided in Resource E. The reason I prefer the unit design approach to standards is that standards are only a framework and do not provide teachers with a coherent plan for addressing standards. Contextualizing standards into teachable units of instruction just makes sense.

2. District Framework in a "Landscape Design" Approach

For school districts that decide to develop core instructional units for the district, but need a "landscape design" with the critical information for district-level use, it is a simple task to "cut and paste" information from the instructional units and put it into a template like that shown in Chart 3.3. This excerpt was drawn from one of the core social studies units in Trenton, New Jersey. A complete social studies unit from Trenton is provided as a model in Resource E2.

Curriculum committees could create a landscape framework using just standards and textbook/curricular materials, but I have found the work is stronger when units are designed first. When teachers have taken the time to think through the flow and depth of their curriculum—unit by unit—they write what students should know, understand, and be able to do with greater clarity and power.

Resource B includes a sample "Curriculum Document Preface" that describes the reasons for moving to a concept-based curriculum and instruction model in a school district. For districts moving in this direction, this introduction can be adapted to fit your work. You are welcome to use and adapt the narrative as a preface for your concept-based curriculum documents.

State and school district academic standards are in various stages of transition toward concept-based designs. Those states and school districts that understand the different levels in the Structure of Knowledge are attending to the conceptual/factual relationships in their designs.

New York, for example, has written a set of core learnings for social studies, Grades K–3, which are beautifully stated conceptual understandings. They need to continue this design process through the grades instead of dropping back into solely fact-based objectives. They will need the factual content as support and foundation, but they will also want to provide teachers with transferable *lessons of history* (deeper, conceptual understandings) related to the factual content in order to engage the intellect beyond memorization. Teaching inductively to these conceptual, enduring understandings facilitates lower-/higher-order synergistic thinking. Intellectual development requires a shift from coverage-centered to idea-centered teaching.

Other states, such as Connecticut and Texas, are moving toward a stronger, conceptual focus for academic standards. They have not arrived in their designs across all disciplines, but they are to be applauded for their direction and tenacity. They are working to meet the intent of state academic standards while maintaining intellectual and instructional integrity.

Curriculum change and instructional change are at once exciting—and painful. Peter Senge et al. quote Richard Beckhard, a leader in organizational change: "People do not resist change; people resist being changed" (1999, p. 14). Change is hard. But teachers and administrators will take on the challenge if they see the value, have quality leadership to pave the way, and feel that the district will stay in the saddle until the job is completed.

SUMMARY

Academic standards are supported by some and cursed by others in the field of education. But standards cannot be ignored in public schools. So the best approach is to recognize their strengths and address their shortfalls.

Chart 3.3   Social Studies Excerpt—Curriculum Framework Template

Unit Title	NJ State Standards	Enduring, Essential Understandings	Guiding Essential Questions	Critical Content	Key Skills	Assessments
Prehistoric Society: Survival		*Students will understand that . . .*		*Students will know . . .*	*Key Skills*	*Assessments*
Length: ___ weeks	6.4A1 6.7B1-2	1. Societies develop technologies to meet their needs.	1a. What is "culture"? b. What kinds of tools were developed in prehistoric societies? c. How were these tools/artifacts used?	• the biological and cultural processes that shaped the earliest human communities. • the early physical and cultural development of humankind from the Paleolithic era to the agricultural revolution and that knowledge of these societies is based on archaeological methods.	• Read maps and translate them into appropriate graphics to display geographic information. • Examine and draw conclusions from artifacts. • Answer geographic questions regarding major physical and human traits. • Compare geographic information presented at different scales.	Investigate prehistoric cultures in order to understand that innovations and chronology cause societies to progress. You are an archaeologist preparing a presentation on the development of prehistoric cultures for an archaeology class. Chart the information from your research on a map and create a colorful and appealing graphic organizer to display the information on prehistoric cultures. Present
	6.4A2 6.3-6	2. Advancing technologies change cultures.	2a. How did the development of early tools/artifacts change prehistoric societies? b. Is change always beneficial? Is change inevitable?			
	6.4A2	3. Artifacts reflect cultural and technological changes.	3a. How do artifacts reflect time, place, and the human condition?			
	6.4A3 6.7B1-2	4. A change from a food-gathering society to an agricultural society leads to a division of labor.	4a. Why did prehistoric societies change from food gatherers to food producers? b. Why did agriculture require a division of labor?	• how early civilizations developed through interactions with their environment.		

Prehistoric Society: Survival		Students will understand that . . .		Students will know . . .	Key Skills	Assessments
			c. How did farming impact the lives of prehistoric peoples? d. Why was the domestication of animals significant to early peoples? e. How do you think the early agricultural societies answered these questions: What to produce? How to produce? For whom?	• how the development of agriculture and trade changed the way ancient peoples lived. • that the earliest peoples banded together to provide for their basic needs and created the first civilizations.	• Hypothesize about the influences of the past on present culture.	your information to the class highlighting the technologies and innovations that allowed the societies to advance.
	6.4A1-3	5. Competition for resources and land can lead to conflict and movement of peoples.	5a. Why does competition for natural resources lead to conflict? b. How can conflict over natural resources lead to the alteration of land boundaries?			
	6.2A5	6. People may form groups to provide for basic needs or for protection.	6a. Why did prehistoric peoples eventually form groups?			

(Continued)

Chart 3.3 (Continued)

Prehistoric Society: Survival	Students will understand that . . .		Students will know . . .	Key Skills	Assessments
6.4A3	7. The resources of a region determine the types of food, clothing, shelter, and tools.	7a. How do groups organize to meet their basic needs? b. What natural resources were available to prehistoric societies? c. How was the first farming done? What tools were used?			
6.4A1	8. The search for resources to meet basic needs influences migration patterns.	8a. Why do groups of people move from one place to another? b. How does geography affect migration patterns?			
6.2A1 6.4A1-2	9. Political systems organize society to maintain order and achieve goals.	9a. Why do societies create political systems, and why do these systems differ across cultures and through time?			
6.4A1-2	10. Civilizations progress socially, economicallly, and politically.	10a. What are the physical and cultural differences between Paleolithic and Neolithic man? How did the Neolithic society develop?			

SOURCE: Rich Howe and Dennis Hillmyer, Trenton Public Schools, Trenton, New Jersey. Used with permission.

This chapter suggests ways to meet the intent of standards while maintaining intellectual and instructional integrity. State standards lack cross-disciplinary design coherence because standards committees at the state level followed the national model for their respective disciplines. The lack of cross-disciplinary coordination at the national level passed on down to the state designs. This chapter suggests that states and school districts can rectify the design problem by bringing a conceptual structure to the design of local standards documents. Science has the strongest design at both the national and state levels because the conceptual structure is apparent. Other disciplines would do well to follow suit. It is confusing to teachers when the various discipline-based standards focus on a different level or type of knowledge, each calling for a different kind of pedagogy.

There are other issues related to standards that confuse teachers. One is the difference between skills and activities. This chapter clarifies the difference. And finally, teachers ask, "How can I possibly meet all these standards?" This chapter suggests that local school districts and teachers can accommodate state standards most effectively if they contextualize those standards into units of instruction. Another option is to create a district-level template in a landscape format for showing the alignment of content, concepts, and skills to the state academic standards.

How teachers approach standards is an indicator of their level of professional expertise. These approaches are characterized in this chapter as novice, practitioner, and expert. We are working to become experts.

Chapter 4 supports teachers further in understanding how to design concept-based units and lessons by addressing some of the components that seem to cause the most confusion.

EXTENDING THOUGHT

1. Academic standards are improving academic achievement. In what ways?

2. Academic standards still need revision. In what ways?

3. Describe the "low-road" approach to standards by classroom teachers.

4. Describe the "high-road" approach to standards by classroom teachers.

5. What obligations do district administrators have in supporting teachers with standards expectations?

6. What obligations do teachers have to help students meet standards expectations?

7. The standards movement is increasing the stress on students and teachers. In what specific ways can schools and school districts help students and teachers manage the stress?

8. In too many school districts, a high percentage of students do not read adequately for middle school and high school work. They face the possibility of being denied a high school diploma. What steps should be taken by the school district administration to address the problem? Create a list of questions that you would ask if you were "auditing" a school or district that had a high percentage of low-performing readers. Now create a list of suggestions to help them improve, based on your projection of their answers.

Designing Concept-Based Units and Lessons

INTERDISCIPLINARY AND INTRADISCIPLINARY UNIT DESIGN: A SHORT PRIMER

Concept-based instructional units can be either interdisciplinary (multiple subjects addressing a common topic) or intradisciplinary (within a specific subject area). What makes them concept based is the conceptual/factual synergy built into the curricular design.

The Unit Components

There are different formats for designing concept-based units, but there are some critical components that appear across all designs.

(Teachers will want to identify and include differentiation strategies to meet the various needs of learners throughout the unit design as appropriate to ensure access for all students to the essential concepts and principles.)

1. **A Unit Title**—The centering topic of study.

2. **A Conceptual Lens**—A broad, integrating concept, or conceptual-level question, that acts as a conceptual filter for students to use in processing factual information. *Lens examples*: *perspective*, *change*, *conflict*, and so on. *Conceptual question*: Is war inevitable? (Without a conceptual focus for content study, the intellectual work for the unit will be shallower.)

3. **Concepts and Subconcepts**—The macro- and microconcepts that give transferable relevance to the study, and that are derived from the critical content.

4. **Generalizations (enduring, essential understandings)**—Five to 12 statements (depending on the grade and readiness level) of transferable, conceptual understandings that are drawn from, and supported by, the critical content.

Because these ideas transfer, they cannot be specific to a time, place, person, or location. These are the significant, conceptual, enduring ideas that students must *understand* at a deeper level as a result of the unit study.

5. **Guiding and Essential Questions**—Questions of different types (e.g., factual, conceptual, or essential [provocative]) that guide student thinking from concrete to abstract levels.

6. **Critical Content**—The factual content which students must *know* to be competent with the topics in the unit.

7. **Key Skills**—Four to eight skills that define what students must be able to *do*. Many teachers confuse these transferable skills with content objectives or activities. Skills are transferable across situations. For example, "Access information using the Internet" is a transferable skill, but "Access information on the Texas Revolution" is an activity. Units should isolate and name the transferable skills that are being taught and then employ those skills in learning experiences and assessments to be certain they are taught and tested.

8. **Performance Tasks and Scoring Guides**—Student performance tasks (two or three) that demonstrate what students must *know*, *understand*, and be able to *do* in the unit. Based on the backward design model of Grant Wiggins and Jay McTighe (1999), teachers design the unit tasks—then design the learning experiences leading up to the performances. The idea is to set students up for success by teaching with the end in mind. In a concept-based, three-dimensional model, the scoring guide addresses criteria describing "quality performance" for conceptual understanding as well as for content knowledge and skills. Too often, the conceptual expectations for performance are missing from the scoring guide. Also plan the other unit assessments (e.g., selected response, essay, or writing prompt) to show evidence of learning.

9. **Learning Experiences**—The unit activities and student performances, supported by teacher lesson plans, that prepare students for success on the performance tasks, and that address the know, understand, and able to do components in the unit. (Note: Though this step *follows* Step 8 [Performance Tasks] in the design process, the instruction *precedes* Step 8 when the unit is implemented.)

10. **Unit Resources/Teacher Notes**—A listing of the needed resources to carry out the unit instruction, and any helpful teacher notes.

Comparing Topic-Based and Concept-Based Units

Figure 4.1 provides a comparison between a traditional, topic-based, two-dimensional unit and a concept-based, three-dimensional unit. Which one provides greater richness and depth? Justify your choice.

Guiding teachers to develop concept-based, three-dimensional units of instruction, like the one in Figure 4.1, is an effective way to support the change to a more intellectually sophisticated model of teaching and learning. There will not be a

(Continued on page 78)

Figure 4.1   Topic-Based Versus Concept-Based Units

	Two-Dimensional Unit: Topic Based	Three-Dimensional Unit: Concept Based
1. Unit Title	**Colonization and Settlement: Beginnings to 1763**	**Colonization and Settlement: Beginnings to 1763**
2. Conceptual Lens	(none)	*Culture/Interactions*
3. Concepts/Subconcepts *Notes: The formal identification of important concepts for the unit provides the "fuel" for writing the deeper enduring, essential understandings.*	(none formally identified)	Colonies, beliefs, customs, values, indigenous peoples, assimilation, cultural identity, social and political structures, trade, goods/services, competition, representative government.
4. Enduring, Essential Understandings (generalizations) *Notes: This is the step that raises the bar for teaching and learning. Concept-based, three-dimensional curriculum and instruction moves beyond traditional objectives focused on the factual input of information to using factual knowledge to gain a deeper understanding of ideas with transferable relevance. These are the "lessons of history." Note that the ideas are statements of conceptual relationship (concepts italicized).*	(none identified—may have lists of content objectives, such as, 4a. "Analyze the factors that led to oversea explorations between the 15th and 17th centuries," and 4b. "Identify the location of the original 13 colonies," or 4c. "Analyze the interactions of the early Spanish, English, French, and Dutch settlers among colonies and with the Native Americans.")	4a. *Nations* explore and establish *colonies* to further their *economic* and *political interests.* 4b. The *cultures* of *indigenous peoples* can be disrupted and dominated by *exploring nations.* 4c. *Colonies* may challenge the *inherited rule* by their *mother country* as they develop *social and political structures* that reinforce their emerging *beliefs* and *values.* 4d. The desire for *products* from other *cultures* stimulates *trade.* 4e. *Prices* for *goods* and *services* fluctuate according to the *level of competition* and *product availability.* 4f. *Basic principles* of *modern government* evolve from a *nation's* early *beliefs, values,* and *experiences.* 4g. *Representative governments* value the *participation* of the *individual citizen* in the *political process.*
5. Guiding/Essential Questions (Samples) *Notes: This is another area of significant difference between topic-based and concept-based units. Topic-based units in history use fact-based questions almost exclusively because the focus is on meeting factual objectives. Concept-based units use three main types of questions: factual, conceptual, and essential (debatable or*	F = factual questions ———————— 5a. What factors led to oversea explorations between the 15th and 17th centuries? (F) What were the key features of the major European explorations during this time? (F) 5b. Where were the 13 colonies located? (F) 5c. What kinds of relationships existed among the Spanish,	F = factual questions, C = conceptual questions, P = provocative questions (debatable, essential) ———————— 5a. What factors led to oversea explorations between the 15th and 17th centuries? (F) 5b. How could the establishment of colonies benefit Spain, England, and France both economically and

(Continued)

Figure 4.1 (Continued)

	Two-Dimensional Unit: Topic Based	Three-Dimensional Unit: Concept Based
provocative). The goal is to use the factual questions to lay a foundation of knowledge, and then ask the conceptual questions to challenge students to bridge in their thinking to the conceptual ideas that have greater depth and transferability.	English, French, and Dutch colonies? (F) 5d. What kinds of relationships existed between the colonial settlers and the Native Americans? (F)	politically during this time of exploration? (F) 5c. Why are nations concerned about economic and political power? (C) 5d. Without the ongoing establishment of colonies, how do nations today make economic and political gains? (C) 5e. Why is there an ongoing "tension" between nations economically and politically? Is this tension healthy or unhealthy? Support your position. (P)
6. Critical Content (required factual knowledge—both units address the required critical content)	6a. The factors that stimulated oversea explorations and the features of the major European explorations between the 15th and 17th centuries. 6b. The cultures and interaction of populations, including patterns of political organization after 1450. 6c. The importance of Islam in Western Africa in the 15th and 16th centuries. 6d. The indigenous cultures in early America, in the Americas, Western Europe, and Africa. 6e. The differences in colonization of the mother countries and the interactions with other colonies and American Indians. 6f. The political, social, and cultural characteristics of the 13 English colonies, including common and distinguishing elements. 6g. The role of religion in the English colonies including governance and relation to the Americas by England, France, and Spain, including Puritanism and the Great Awakening.	6a. The factors that stimulated oversea explorations and the features of the major European explorations between the 15th and 17th centuries. 6b. The cultures and interaction of populations, including patterns of political organization after 1450. 6c. The importance of Islam in Western Africa in the 15th and 16th centuries. 6d. The indigenous cultures in early America, in the Americas, Western Europe, and Africa. 6e. The differences in colonization of the mother countries and the interactions with other colonies and American Indians. 6f. The political, social, and cultural characteristics of the 13 English colonies, including common and distinguishing elements. 6g. The role of religion in the English colonies including governance and relation to the Americas by England, France, and Spain, including Puritanism and the Great Awakening.
7. Key Skills (the same in both units) *Note: When these skills are attached to specific content in the design of instructional*	7a. Display and analyze historical information using a graphic organizer. 7b. Use decision-making skills to take positions on controversial	7a. Display and analyze historical information using a graphic organizer. 7b. Use decision-making skills to take positions on controversial

	Two-Dimensional Unit: Topic Based	Three-Dimensional Unit: Concept Based
activities, differentiation strategies can be employed to meet individual and group needs. For example, the skill can be applied to more complex or less complex material, or the expectations for skill performance can be set at greater or less sophisticated levels.	issues based on critical analysis of the information or positions presented. 7c. Formulate questions and search for answers by conducting historical research. 7d. Critically analyze printed materials to identify bias, point of view, and context. 7e. Create a map to show the location of historical sites. 7f. Use multimedia technology to share historical information.	issues based on critical analysis of the information or positions presented. 7c. Formulate questions and search for answers by conducting historical research. 7d. Critically analyze printed materials to identify bias, point of view, and context. 7e. Create a map to show the location of historical sites. 7f. Use multimedia technology to share historical information.
8. Performance Task *Notes: Though these performance tasks look the same, there is a significant difference:* *The focus for the two-dimensional task is having students answer factual questions related to the 13 colonies.* *The focus for the three-dimensional task is having students answer questions that demonstrate two of the enduring, essential understandings in addition to the basic factual knowledge questions.* *Critical to this difference is the task design. Notice that the two-dimensional model gives students very little direction in developing the colonies questions.* *The teacher designing the three-dimensional model has chosen two enduring understandings (the "why") from the unit under study (the "what"). Once the teacher had identified the "what" and the "why," it was a simple task to pick up some of the language from the "why" statement and build it into the "how" (the Engaging Scenario). You can see how this tip works by comparing the italicized material. The "what" and "why"*	(Engaging Scenario) 8a. You are the creative designer for Gameboards America. You have been charged with designing a game to teach eighth graders about the original 13 colonies of early America. 1. Identify the purpose of your game. 2. Develop a set of at least 30 "Colonies Questions" with answers on the reverse side. 3. Design the game board so that players move along a path from Start to Finish by correctly answering a Colonies Question. (Draw a rough draft of the game board on a piece of paper.) 4. Place seven "Penalty" and seven "Bonus" points along the game path, and develop Penalty and Bonus cards. (Place the cards in Penalty and Bonus boxes somewhere on the game board.) 5. Decide how the players will move through the game for correct answers (dice, spinner, or number of moves noted on the answer card). 6. Find or make chips or tokens to use as playing pieces. 7. Transfer the rough draft to card stock or cardboard and use marking pens for color. 8. Play the game to test it!	8a. **What (the unit study):** Investigate early cultures, colonization, and settlement (beginnings to 1763) . . . **Why (the enduring understandings):** In order to understand that *nations explore and establish colonies to further their economic and political interests;* and that *cultures are shaped by historical events, traditions, values, and beliefs.* **How (Engaging Scenario):** You are the creative designer for Gameboards America. You have been charged with designing a game to teach eighth graders about the original 13 colonies of early America. 1. Identify the purpose of your game. 2. Develop a set of at least 30 "Colonies Questions" with answers on the reverse side. *Include questions on why the European nations set up the colonies, as well as questions on the political, social (include the role of religion), and economic characteristics of the different colonies. Include the following question with your answer on the reverse side of the card: "How did historical events (option—values and beliefs) shape the culture of Jamestown?"* 3. Design the game board so that players move along a path from

(Continued)

Figure 4.1 (Continued)

	Two-Dimensional Unit: Topic Based	Three-Dimensional Unit: Concept Based
statements are for the teacher in planning; the students get the "how" scenario.		Start to Finish by correctly answering a Colonies Question. (Draw a rough draft of the game board on a piece of paper.)
		(Steps 4–8 are the same as in the two-dimensional unit.)
9. Learning Experiences *Notes: The topic-based experiences focus again on knowing information. Notice the greater intellectual challenge in the concept-based learning experiences. The incorporation of conceptual expectations engages the personal intellect and increases student motivation for learning.* **Notes on Differentiation of Curriculum and Instruction:** *All children (except those with a special educational plan [IEP] indicating otherwise) are required to comprehend and apply the enduring, essential understandings and the critical content, as well as to develop the key skills. But how teachers bring students to these competencies can vary based on learner needs.* *The first learning experience in the concept-based unit provides suggestions for differentiating instruction. See if you can identify differentiation strategies for the learning experiences numbered 2–4.*	9a. Read textbook Chapter 2 on Early American colonization. Answer questions at the end of the chapter. 9b. Draw a map of the 13 colonies on 12" × 18" paper. Cut the map into a jigsaw puzzle and trade with a partner. Try to put the puzzle together in five minutes. 9c. Create a graphic organizer to compare the 13 colonies: ♦ mother country ♦ reason for colonization ♦ economies ♦ customs/traditions ♦ religions ♦ leadership	9a. **Standard Level 2:** Use primary and secondary source documents found through teacher-provided Web sites to compare accounts of European colonization in early America. Create a graphic organizer with the following comparisons: ♦ Mother country ♦ Reasons for colonization ♦ Political/social/economic characteristics of the colonies (three columns) Summarize your comparisons in a well-constructed paragraph. *See Differentiation Strategies for Readiness Levels 1 and 3 in the box below this chart.* 9b. Fold a piece of 12" × 18" paper in half like a book. Draw a map of the 13 colonies on the left side of the paper. Draw a map of western Europe showing Spain, England, France, and the Netherlands during the late 1700s. Using colored markers and a ruler, draw the connection between the mother country and her colonies. On the connecting line for each mother country and colony, neatly write a word that conveys a strong influence on the development of the colony (e.g., beliefs/values, leadership, events). 9c. Use one of the unit lenses— *culture* or *interactions*—to reflect on one or more of the colonies. You need to convey one aspect of the "culture" of your colony, or you need to convey the idea of "interaction" between two or more cultures. Your creative reflection can be in one of the following forms:

	Two-Dimensional Unit: Topic Based	Three-Dimensional Unit: Concept Based
		◆ Poem
		◆ Visual display (on paper or computer)
		◆ Song
		◆ Dance
		◆ Story (oral or written)
		9d. Create a "minigame" on an 8½" × 11" sheet of paper. Your minigame has to focus on any one of the concepts we are studying in this unit (trade, competition, culture, assimilation, etc.). Be ready to explain to a partner how your game reflects your concept.
		Note: Additional learning experiences address the other enduring, essential understandings; critical content knowledge; and skills identified for this unit.
10. Teacher Resources and Teacher Notes	Chapter 2—history textbook	Decide whether to have each individual student or teams build the game board. If a team develops the game board, each student must be responsible for developing a certain number of question cards and answers.

Note: Even though we are differentiating tasks based on the readiness levels of students, we expect the same understanding of key concepts and enduring understandings.

Differentiation for Readiness Level 1 and Level 3 (Level 2 is the standard):

Level 1: Provide Web sites with easier readability for primary and secondary source documents. If necessary, underline (without specifying) the political, social, and economic characteristics in the printed Web site material. Then have students determine and highlight political characteristics with one color, and social and economic characteristics in two other colors. Provide a blank graphic organizer and have them fill the highlighted information in the correct columns.
Ask students to discuss their findings with a partner, then write at least four sentences describing their comparisons.

Level 3: Using appropriate search engines and key words, students locate primary and secondary source documents, design an appropriate graphic organizer, and enter the required information. Ask students to, in two well-constructed paragraphs,
a. describe the findings of their comparison, and
b. analyze the similarities and differences between the early colonies and our community today.

Challenge question:
Which of the following do you think has had the greatest impact on the development of civilization?
◆ Transportation
◆ Technology
◆ Creative thinking
◆ Communication
Defend and support your position.

significant improvement in education until teachers (and administrators) understand the importance of concepts and conceptual understanding to intellectual development, deeper understanding, and student motivation for learning. This book hopes to provide the background information that educators need to make a shift toward the following ideas:

♦ The difference between a topic and a concept and between a fact and a generalization
♦ The importance of teaching to transferable, conceptual ideas using the facts as the supporting foundation rather than covering objectives with little thought
♦ How to design units and lessons that support three-dimensional, concept-based teaching and learning

We cannot assume that teachers have this information—nor can we just exhort them to "do it." They need specific information and guidance to follow this path.

I touched on the issue of differentiation of curriculum and instruction in the design of the unit in Figure 4.1. Carol Ann Tomlinson and I have discussed the critical importance of concepts and enduring understandings to differentiation of curriculum and instruction. We believe that when teachers do not construct curriculum around concepts and understandings, they tend to "differentiate" by giving students more or less work based on their ability. They vary the quantity of work—a poor interpretation of the meaning of differentiation. If teachers understand that all students need to have a deep understanding of concepts and enduring understandings, however, it gives them the insight for quality differentiation. They ask the question, "How can I design the curricular and instructional experiences to help each student attain the key concepts and understandings using the critical content?" Concept-based instruction puts virtually all children—including special education, gifted, and second language learners—on the playing field of learning and enhances each child's opportunity for a touchdown.

Planning Units for a Year

Teachers, or curriculum committees, can plan effectively for the year's work by designing *overview webs* of the core instructional units prior to designing the full units. Steps 1–3 of the unit components just described are placed on the unit web along with key topics. (The webs only identify the critical content topics and concepts for a unit; the skills are brought into the unit at a later point.) Completing the unit webs for the year as a first step provides certain benefits:

♦ The critical content topics and concepts from the state academic standards can be contextualized onto the unit webs at the appropriate instructional points.
♦ The unit web gives an overview of the breadth and depth of required instruction.

Figure 4.2

SOURCE: David Ford Cartoons, davidford@cablespeed.com. Used with permission.

♦ Doing the unit webs for the year provides teachers with a reassurance that they can accomplish the required curriculum once they determine where the content fits.
♦ The unit webs allow the teacher to control standards-driven curriculum in a reasonable and workable way. The textbook and the standards are a resource. The instructional units are the curriculum.

Figures 4.3a–c provide a few sample webs from a middle school world history course. Notice that the key topics and concepts correlate by number to the state academic standards. These samples were developed by Rich Howe and Dennis Hillmyer in the Trenton Public School District, Trenton, New Jersey.

Alan Rudig and Dave Holze, secondary mathematics teachers from Chilton, Wisconsin, decided to web the trigonometry concepts they would be addressing across three courses: Geometry, Advanced Mathematics I, and Advanced Mathematics II. Figure 4.4 shares their web.

Once the web was completed, Dave and Alan were able to write mathematics generalizations for the three courses to reflect the trigonometry understandings:

(Continued on page 83)

Figure 4.3a Prehistoric Society Unit Web

Unit Planner

Critical Content/Concept Web

Unit Title: Prehistoric Society: Survival

Conceptual Lens: Change & Survival

Unit Title

Prehistoric Society: Survival

Unit Overview

How would you have liked living in prehistoric times?

Imagine what it would have been like to rely on your inventiveness just to survive!

In this unit we will see how prehistoric people discovered and used fire to meet their needs; how they developed language to communicate; and how they used the environment to create tools.

We will learn how prehistoric people advanced from food gatherers to food producers; and how specialization, government and religion shaped early societies.

Grade Level: 6

6.4A1-2* **Culture**
- ◆ Artifacts
- ◆ Paleolithic (Old Stone Age)
- ◆ Neolithic (New Stone Age)

6.4A2 **History**
- ◆ History before written language (prehistory)
- ◆ Pictographs (drawn)
- ◆ Petroglyphs (chiseled)
- ◆ Timeline

6.I7B1 **Economics**
- ◆ Division of labor
- ◆ Revolution of agriculture

6.2B1 **Government**
- ◆ Tribes
- ◆ Clans
- ◆ Family unit
- ◆ Small farms

6.4A3 **Geography**
6.8E6
- ◆ Human-environmental interaction – available resources; uses
- ◆ Movement of people (hunter-gatherers follow the food supply)

* Numbers on the web correlate to the New Jersey Core Content Standards.

SOURCE: Rich Howe and Dennis Hillmyer, Trenton Public Schools, Trenton, New Jersey. Used with permission.

Figure 4.3b River Valley Civilizations Unit Web

Unit Planner

Critical Content/Concept Web

Unit Title: River Valley Civilizations

Conceptual Lens: Interactions

Unit Overview

Why did early civilizations flourish in the River Valley? Why was water so important to the development of early civilizations?

In this unit we will take a tour of the River Valley Civilizations. We will see how civilizations developed and revolved around religion and family life. We'll see how the government structured the society and how interactions between people led to a change in laws.

Grade Level: 6

6.4A1* **Culture**
  ♦ Religion
  6.9A4 ♦ Development
  6.9C1   of language
  ♦ Social Structure
     (hierarchy)
  ♦ Migration

6.2A1 **Government**
  ♦ Rulers
  ♦ Laws
  ♦ Hierarchy
  ♦ Transfer of power

6.4A4 **History**
  ♦ Mesopotamia
  ♦ Egypt
  ♦ China
  ♦ India
  ♦ Phoenicians
  ♦ Babylonians
  ♦ Assyrians
  ♦ Hebrews

Unit Title

River Valley Civilizations: Interactions

6.9,3,4 **Economics**
  ♦ Specialization
  6.7B1,2 ♦ Use of resources
  ♦ Trade
  ♦ Slavery
  ♦ Transfer of land

6.4A3 **Geography**
  6.8E6 ♦ Regions
  ♦ Human/
     environmental
     interactions
  ♦ Movement
     of peoples

* Numbers on the web correlate to the New Jersey Core Content Standards.

SOURCE: Rich Howe and Dennis Hillmyer, Trenton Public Schools, Trenton, New Jersey. Used with permission.

Figure 4.3c Greece and Rome Unit Web

Critical Content/Concept Web

Unit Planner

Unit Title: Greece and Rome ... Classical Traditions

Conceptual Lens: Origins & Contributions

Unit Overview

Throughout the world, we can see the cultural contributions from early Greece and Rome. From stately columns and lions' heads that convey the power of large buildings, to the origins of the Olympics in sports, we experience the contributions of classical civilizations.

In this unit we will discover the cultures of early Greece and Rome and follow their contributions to the world of today—in art, architecture, ideas, and sports.

6.9A4   **Culture**
6.3A2   ◆ Language
6.4B2,3 ◆ Religion
         ◆ Fine arts
         ◆ Architecture
         ◆ Sports
         ◆ Philosophers
         ◆ Literature

6.7B1,2* **Economics**
6.4B2,3   ◆ Merchandising
          ◆ Trade
          ◆ Colonization
          ◆ Expansion

6.4B2,3 **History**
         ◆ Greece
         ◆ Rome

6.4B2,3 **Government**
6.2B2   ◆ Democracy
6.2A3   ◆ Oligarchy
         ◆ Republic

Unit Title

**Greece and Rome ...
Classical Traditions:
Origins & Contributions**

6.8E1,6 **Geography**
         ◆ Space
         ◆ Place
         ◆ Location
         ◆ Human/Environmental
           Interactions

Grade Level: 6

* Numbers on the web correlate to the New Jersey Core Content Standards.

SOURCE: Rich Howe and Dennis Hillmyer, Trenton Public Schools, Trenton, New Jersey. Used with permission.

Figure 4.4 Trigonometry Web

Conceptual Lens: Relationships

FUNCTIONS
- Sine
- Cos
- Tan
- Csc
- Sec
- Cot
- Inverses
- Domain
- Range

RIGHT TRIANGLE
- Opposite
- Adjacent
- Hypotenuse
- Similarity

FORMULAS
- Pythagorean Theorem
- Pythagorean Identity
- Tangent
- Law of Cosines
- Law of Sines
- Area of Triangle
- Double Angles
- Half Angles

TRIGONOMETRY

ANGLES
- Degree
- Minute
- Second
- Radian
- Depression
- Elevation

GRAPHS
- Unit Circle
- Coordinate Plane
- Symmetry
- Polar Coordinates
- Asymptotes

FRACTIONS
- Proportions
- Equations

TRANSFORMATIONS
- Amplitude
- Vertical Shift
- Phase Shift
- Period

SOURCE: From "Trigonometry: Mathematical Concept Web and Generalizations," unit developed by Alan Rudig and Dave Holze, Chilton High School, Wisconsin. Used with permission.

(Continued from page 79)

Sample Trigonometry Generalizations and Guiding Questions

Level 1: *Geometry* **(Wisconsin Math Standards)**

Similar triangles share the same proportions. (B.12.2, C.12.3, D.12.3)
▶ How can we prove that triangles are similar?
▶ What does it mean to be proportional?

Right triangles define trigonometric functions. (C.12.5)
▶ How do the sides of a right triangle relate to the trigonometric functions?
▶ How do you know when a side is adjacent and when it is opposite?

Depression and elevation determine angles in a triangle. (C.12.2)
▶ What is the difference between angle depression and elevation?
▶ What effect does a change in elevation or depression have?

Fractions express trigonometric ratios. (C.12.5)
▶ How are the ratios of the sides affected by the angles?

(Continued)

(Continued)

Formulas can determine unknown sides and angles. (C.12.5)
- ▶ Why would you need to know an unknown angle or side?
- ▶ What information is necessary to use a trigonometry formula?

Trigonometry solves real-life problems. (C.12.2, E.12.1, F.12.4)
- ▶ Where do you find right triangles in the real world?
- ▶ Which professions use angles?

Level 2: *Advanced Math Concepts I and II*

Degrees and radians define angle measures.
- ▶ What is the relationship among degrees, radians, and revolutions?

Transformations affect graphs and equations. (C.12.1, F.12.1, F.12.2)
- ▶ What types of transformations can be applied to an equation?
- ▶ How do amplitude, period, phase shift, and vertical shift affect the graph?

There are formulas that express the numerous relationships among the trigonometric functions. (D.12.3)
- ▶ What is a unit circle?
- ▶ How do sine and cosine relate in terms of a unit circle?
- ▶ How do sine and cosine relate in terms of tangent?

Angles can be trigonometrically equivalent.
- ▶ Are all angles unique?
- ▶ Why do angles share the same coordinates on a unit circle?

Rotation determines angle sign.
- ▶ How does a mathematician distinguish between clockwise and counterclockwise rotations?

Level 3: *Advanced Math Concepts II* **only**

Trigonometric functions can be graphed in Cartesian and polar coordinates systems. (C.12.4)
- ▶ Why would you consider more than one graphing system?
- ▶ What advantages do the different coordinate systems have?

Webbing is a powerful tool in designing concept-based curriculum because it allows teachers to see an overview of the critical topics, concepts, and subconcepts for their work. The more complete the planning web, the stronger the enduring, essential understandings.

Instead of a concept web, some districts choose to use a flow chart to identify macroconcepts and subconcepts to overview their work. The flow chart is then used to write the enduring, essential understandings.

Figure 4.5 shows a concept flow chart for elementary physical education developed by teachers in the Meridian School District, Meridian, Idaho.

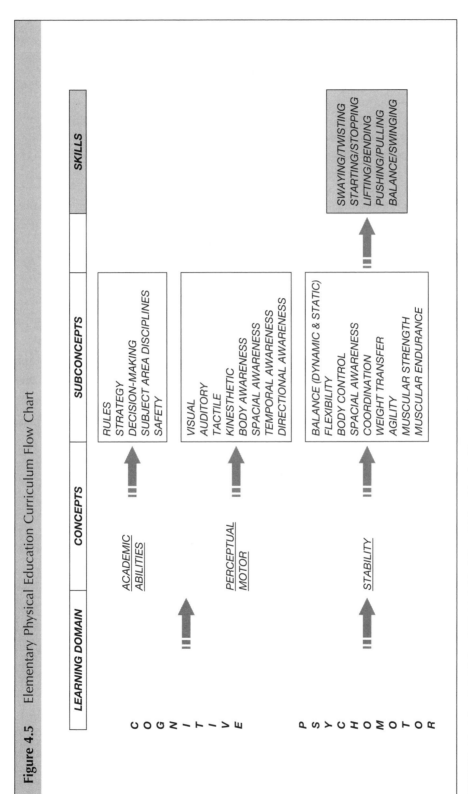

Figure 4.5   Elementary Physical Education Curriculum Flow Chart

LEARNING DOMAIN	CONCEPTS	SUBCONCEPTS	SKILLS

C O G N I T I V E

ACADEMIC ABILITIES

RULES
STRATEGY
DECISION-MAKING
SUBJECT AREA DISCIPLINES
SAFETY

PERCEPTUAL MOTOR

VISUAL
AUDITORY
TACTILE
KINESTHETIC
BODY AWARENESS
SPACIAL AWARENESS
TEMPORAL AWARENESS
DIRECTIONAL AWARENESS

P S Y C H O M O T O R

STABILITY

BALANCE (DYNAMIC & STATIC)
FLEXIBILITY
BODY CONTROL
SPACIAL AWARENESS
COORDINATION
WEIGHT TRANSFER
AGILITY
MUSCULAR STRENGTH
MUSCULAR ENDURANCE

SWAYING/TWISTING
STARTING/STOPPING
LIFTING/BENDING
PUSHING/PULLING
BALANCE/SWINGING

SOURCE: Meridian Joint School District, Meridian, Idaho. Used with permission.

CREATING LESSON PLANS

Activities Versus Performances

The design of lesson plans by the teacher to carry out the unit work is just as critical to concept-based learning as the overall unit design. In fact, from my review of teaching units and lesson plans in districts that are transitioning to a concept-based model, a breakdown often occurs at the lesson plan level. Educators on the concept-based journey are writing beautiful enduring, essential understandings for their instructional units, but examination of the specific lessons and performance tasks finds that the lesson design more often than not falls short of the conceptual understandings. In this section, we will explore the design of quality performances that reflect what Javier and Kelly *understand,* as well as what they *know.*

Quality lesson plans meet certain criteria. They are

- ◆ *coherent*—There is a clear link between what students must know (factually), understand (conceptually), and be able to do (skillfully).
- ◆ *interesting*—The lesson is motivating to students. They want to participate.
- ◆ *time-worthy*—The lesson is worth the time spent.
- ◆ *standards aligned*—The lesson supports the deeper intent of academic standards (the often-implied conceptual intent) as well as the factual and skill-based expectations.
- ◆ *differentiated*—The lesson meets the learning needs of different kinds of learners to maximize successful learning.

Instructional units have clear statements of what students must know, understand, and be able to do, but the lesson plans too often may lack coherence to the expectations—especially to the enduring understandings. Instructional activities included in a lesson plan have students use skills to learn factual content—but then the lesson often stops, rather than requiring students to bridge to the transferable understandings. This problem is especially egregious in history instruction. Let me show you what I mean.

Read through the following student activity from a lesson on the American Revolution.

Student Activity:

Research primary and secondary source documents related to the causes of the American Revolution. Write a three-page summary of the causes. Include information on the significant historical figures, dates, and events provided by the teacher.

The activity is topic based (two-dimensional). That is, there is no expectation that the students will demonstrate a transferable, conceptual understanding. Before you read further, see if you can figure out how you would adapt the activity to make it concept based. (Hint: You will need to develop a transferable idea [generalization] that can move student thinking beyond the facts—"The students understand that. . . .")

To change an activity into a concept-based performance, teachers can use the Performance Planning Chart (see Chart 4.1) by Lael Williams, Washington state curriculum consultant. As one example, the chart takes the previous student activity and adds a conceptual understanding dimension. Students must perform with, and beyond, the facts to a deeper level of understanding. Correlating the *know*, *understand*, and able to *do* components from an instructional unit ensures that all components are addressed and moves a lower-level *activity* into a *performance* of deeper, conceptual understanding. The teacher also considers how to differentiate for different kinds of learners.

Chart 4.1   Performance Planning Chart

KNOW the . . .	UNDERSTAND That . . .	Able to DO	Student Performance	Differentiation
. . . causes of the American Revolution.	. . . perspectives based on strongly held beliefs and values can lead to conflict and/or revolution.	♦ Research and use primary and secondary source documents to support a position. ♦ Debate a position using effective debate skills.	Select your role as a Tory or Patriot in the American Revolution. Prepare to debate your opponent on the issues by researching primary and secondary source documents related to the causes of the American Revolution. Support your chosen perspective with reasoned argument based on your character's beliefs and values.	♦ Provide source documents at the appropriate reading level; students use highlighters to mark the causes of the Revolution. ♦ Options for debate: a. Give an oral presentation to your Tory or Patriot friends telling why you believe in your position on the issues. b. Draw a picture or cartoon illustrating a Tory or Patriot position on one of the issues.

SOURCE: Lael Williams, curriculum consultant, Edmonds, Washington. Used with permission.

Notice that the student performance picks up some of the language from the conceptual understanding to ensure that this dimension is addressed. This tip helps ensure that your students perform to the level of deep understanding. Teachers also want to help students make connections to other conflicts they may have studied that were based on differing perspectives shaped by strong emotions or beliefs (the North and the South during the Civil War, the War on Terrorism, etc.).

You might be thinking that it is more important to know the causes of the American Revolution (solid, significant facts), than to dilly-dally around with ideas like beliefs and values (nebulous, feely stuff). But don't miss the point—when students are required to think about facts through a conceptual lens such as *per-spectives*, they are bringing their own higher-order thinking to the study. Their thinking is synergistic and personal. They are constructing meaning and finding relevance. And they will be able to transfer knowledge.

The teacher planning the lesson in Chart 4.1 also considered ways to meet the needs of delayed learners by differentiating ways of demonstrating understanding. Notice, however, that the differentiated performances still expect demonstration of the same content knowledge and conceptual understanding.

Differentiation

Carol Ann Tomlinson is "Dr. Differentiation" in my book (figuratively and fondly). It is enlightening and motivating to hear her speak about honoring each student's learning needs and maximizing each student's learning capacity. Certainly, it would appear to be much easier in the short run to "deliver" knowledge to students as if they were a set of empty mailboxes sitting in the post office waiting to be filled. But they are not mailboxes, and they are not empty. And our job is not to deliver but to reach, teach, and engage.

Tomlinson and Eidson (2003b, p. 3) provide a wealth of material to help us meet the diverse needs of our students. They remind us that students' "readiness for the learning, their interests (a motivating hook for engaging them in learning), and their learning profile (ways they learn best) are important considerations as a teacher plans for instruction." Tomlinson and Eidson (2003b, p. 3) share five classroom elements that can be differentiated or modified:

- *Content*—The subject matter and skills
- *Process*—How students create a personal connection to what they must know, understand, and be able to do
- *Products*—The evidence for what students know, understand, and are able to do
- *Affect*—The synergy between thought and emotions
- *Learning environment*—The classroom "climate" and operating procedures

In addition to *Differentiation in Practice: A Resource Guide for Differentiating Curriculum* for Grades K–5 and 5–9, by Tomlinson and Eidson (2003a & b), the Association for Supervision and Curriculum Development has published a third book in this series for Grades 9–12 by Tomlinson and Strickland (2005).

PERFORMANCES VERSUS ACTIVITIES

Now that we are clear on how to build a strong performance and have considered the elements for differentiating curriculum and instruction, let's take the little quiz in the series of boxes in Figure 4.6. Tell whether each of the following learning experiences, built from the state academic standard and a related enduring understanding, is a performance or an activity. For items identified as activities, see if you can add something to make them into a performance. As you work to change lower-level activities into quality student performances, consider these design questions:

Figure 4.6   Performance/Activity Quiz

---

1. State Academic Standard:

"Analyze Lincoln's ideas about liberty, equality, union, and government as contained in his first and second inaugural address and the Gettysburg Address."

Enduring Understanding (generalization):

Watershed events mark turning points in history.

Performance or Activity?

Recite from memory key passages from the Gettysburg Address.

---

2. State Academic Standard:

"Analyze the causes and effects of physical and human geographic factors on major historical and contemporary events in the United States."

Enduring Understanding (generalization):

The availability of human and material resources provides tactical advantages in times of war.

Performance or Activity?

Create pie graphs that show available resources to the North and South before the Civil War.

---

3. State Academic Standard:

"Identify the reasons for and describe the system of checks and balances outlined in the U.S. Constitution."

(Continued)

Figure 4.6 (Continued)

Enduring Understanding (generalization):

The values, beliefs, and ideals of a country are reflected in its laws and political documents.

Performance or Activity?

Design a graphic organizer demonstrating the U.S. system of checks and balances. Then have students use the graphic organizer to write a rationale defending why they think the system of checks and balances reflects American values and beliefs.

4. State Academic Standard:

"Identify the influence of ideas from historic documents including the Magna Carta, the English Bill of Rights, the Mayflower Compact, the Declaration of Independence, the Federalist Papers, and selected anti-federalist writings on the U.S. system of government."

Enduring Understanding (generalization):

Political documents can set forth social ideals such as justice, equality, or freedom, but the path to ideals is impeded by conflicting notions.

Performance or Activity?

Create an outline highlighting social ideas such as justice, equality, or freedom for the Magna Carta, the English Bill of Rights, the Mayflower Compact, the Declaration of Independence, the Federalist Papers, and selected anti-federalist writings on the U.S. Constitution. Select one of these social ideas and describe how conflicting notions have impeded the progress of these ideals.

(Cite specific examples from history or current events to support your position.)

5. State Academic Standard:

"Explain the impact of significant international events such as World War I and World War II on changes in the role of government."

"Predict the effects of selected contemporary legislation on the roles of government."

Enduring Understanding (generalization)

As a society becomes more complex, the role of government increases in the daily lives of its citizens.

Performance or Activity?

Create a three-column chart. In the first column, list significant international events such as World War I, World War II, and global terrorism. In the second column, show some of the resulting U.S. legislation, or governmental policies, enacted in response to these events. In the third column, detail the impact of the legislation on the daily lives of citizens. In a paragraph below the chart, answer this question: "How does the increasing complexity (social, economic, and political) of a society lead to the expansion of government?"

1. Did your performance meet all three components (know/understand/do)?

2. Did you build some of the "understanding" (generalization) language into the performance to ensure the mental bridging to the deeper idea?

3. Did your performance meet the criteria for a quality lesson plan described earlier in this chapter?

After you take the quiz, you can check your answers in Figure 4.7.

Now challenge yourself and figure out ways to differentiate the performances according to one or more of the elements suggested by Tomlinson and Eidson (2003b).

QUESTIONS AND ANSWERS ON UNIT AND LESSON DESIGN

As teachers work in designing concept-based units and lessons, questions continue to arise. This section addresses some of those concerns:

1. How can I identify appropriate concepts for my grade level or course?

Answer: The state academic standards provide many of the concepts that are required at your grade level. You will need to know the difference between a specific topic and a concept, however, to discriminate in the standards. In most states, your science standards are replete with concepts so the job is easier; but the history standards are topic based, and you will have to draw out the implied concepts.

Figure 4.7   Answers: Performance/Activity Quiz

1. An activity—we need to add some language from the enduring understanding to create a performance.

Student Performance:

Recite from memory key passages from the Gettysburg Address. Tell why Lincoln's Gettysburg Address is considered a watershed event in American history. Or, explain why Lincoln's ideas about liberty, equality, union, and government are critical to an understanding of American democracy today.

Differentiation: _____

_____

2. An activity—we need to add a step to reach the enduring understanding.

Student Performance:

Create pie graphs that show available resources to the North and South before the Civil War, and describe how resources can affect the outcome of a war.

Differentiation: _____

_____

3. A performance because it reaches the conceptual depth of the enduring understanding.

Differentiation: _____

_____

4. A performance because it reaches the conceptual depth of the enduring understanding.

Differentiation: _____

_____

5. A performance because it reaches the conceptual depth of the enduring understanding.

Differentiation: _____

_____

Also—trust your own abilities to identify the concepts for your grade or course. If you know the difference between a topic and a concept, sit down with a piece of paper and list the major topics you teach in a subject, and then brainstorm the concepts that you work with under each of those topics.

For secondary teachers—dig deep into your microconcepts. The microconcepts are what differentiate the depth of knowledge that you are teaching from that taught in the elementary grade levels. In the intermediate grade levels, we teach about ecosystems, habitats, predators, and prey. But in secondary schools, we deal with such specific concepts as niches, parasitism, and commensalism. The generalizations you teach toward need to use the specific concepts to develop increasing conceptual depth in a student's understanding.

2. What tips do you have for writing clear and powerful generalizations?

Answer: When people first begin writing the enduring, essential understandings, they are often very general and obtuse. The overuse of the verbs *impact*, *affect*, and, *influence*, as well as the verbs *is*, *are*, and *have*, is a major reason for these weak statements. Learning how to scaffold your thinking using questions is a powerful tool for tightening, clarifying, and developing generalizations to deeper levels of sophistication. To scaffold a generalization from a weaker Level 1, use and answer the questions "How?" "Why?" and "So what?" Read through the following example of a scaffolded generalization from the bottom up (Level 1 to Level 3):

> *Level 3:* Severe disruption of a community's social and economic infrastructure leads to feelings of loss, anxiety, confusion, and anger. Or, severe disruption of a community's social and economic infrastructure requires strong leadership with the ability to problem solve, communicate effectively, and collaborate to get things done.
>
> *So what*—is the significance, or effect, if the social and economic infrastructure is disrupted?
>
> *Level 2:* Natural disasters can disrupt the social and economic infrastructure of a community.
>
> *How* do natural disasters impact a community?
>
> *Level 1:* Natural disasters impact a community.

Note that we want to drop the weaker Level 1 generalizations in our units and teach to Level 2. Teaching to this level will raise academic standards because we are teaching to deeper, conceptual specificity. Level 3 can be used to differentiate and challenge advanced learners, or you may wish to take all students through to Level 3.

Here are some additional scaffolding samples from a ninth grade physics unit on constant acceleration developed by Matt Watson and Cathy Harne, Twin Valley School District, Elverson, Pennsylvania:

Level 3: The velocity of an object can be determined from an x-t graph even if the x-t graph is curved.

So what is the significance?

Level 2: By drawing secant chords and solving for the slope of the chord, one can determine the instantaneous velocity of the object at an intermediate clock reading.

How does the slope determine the velocity?

Level 1: The slope of an x-t graph can determine the velocity of an object.

3. How many units should I teach in a year?

Answer: Rule of thumb—for elementary grades, three or four social studies–based units; three or four science-based units (then create interdisciplinarity by bringing other subjects, like art, music, and literature, into the unit); for secondary courses, five to eight instructional units for a yearlong course.

4. Why do you think lesson plans and teaching have traditionally failed to reach the deeper level of conceptual understanding?

Answer: This answer is easy—we have not had a concept-based curriculum design. We have not formally identified and written into our curriculum documents the conceptual ideas (enduring understandings) that give relevance to the fact base. We desperately need idea-centered curricula and idea-centered teaching to develop greater intelligence.

5. Will concept-based instruction make my job as a teacher easier or harder?

Answer: Though there will be some new learning and curriculum adaptation up front, the payoff for both teachers and students will be significant:
Students will

♦ retain factual information longer;
♦ develop conceptual depth of knowledge through the grades and will find patterns, connections, and relevance to their own lives; and
♦ be motivated to use their personal intellect.

Teachers will

♦ have clear and powerful conceptual understandings to teach toward—this will allow them to focus the use of their factual content;
♦ deepen their understanding of the discipline(s) they teach as they continually relate the factual knowledge to the conceptual understandings; and
♦ realize that the concepts and generalizations do not have to be totally "rewritten" every time a curriculum adoption comes around—because concepts and generalizations are timeless constructs.

Questions will continue to arise on a concept-based journey, but questions challenge us to extend our thinking and guide our performance in the art, science, and craft of teaching.

SUMMARY

This chapter briefly discusses concept-based unit design and shares a set of design steps that correlate with the unit planner in Resource E2. Sample overview webs for units support a discussion on planning a subject area curriculum for a year. The major focus for this chapter, however, addresses the difference between lower-level activities and more complex performances in lesson design. Too often, instructional activities fail to reach the level of a quality performance. Quality performances require students to demonstrate enduring, conceptual understandings, as well as content knowledge and skills. This chapter presents a quiz to help teachers differentiate between an activity and a performance.

Chapter 5 moves us into the area of three-dimensional, concept-based instruction. It is the instruction that shows the teacher's knowledge of the art and science of teaching. It is the instruction that each child uses as a springboard for developing intelligence.

EXTENDING THOUGHT

1. Why should we spend time designing instructional units for the year when a textbook "has it all"?

2. What is the difference between a traditional, topic-based unit and a concept-based unit?

3. How can we use unit overview webs to contextualize the state academic standards?

4. How does a concept-based unit support
   a. teaching for deep understanding,
   b. the transfer of knowledge, and
   c. the development of intelligence?

5. What is the difference between an activity and a performance?

6. Can you take the following activity and turn it into a performance?

Activity: Go to the museum and view ancient Egyptian artifacts.

*Performance:*_____

_____

7. What steps did you have to take to make this change from an activity to a performance? How could you differentiate your performance to meet the different learning needs of students?

8. What question do *you* have regarding concept-based unit and lesson design? Write your inner dialogue on the question, then pair with a colleague and try to reach some consensus on the answer.

Concept-Based Instruction

C oncept-based curriculum and instruction requires a shift in classroom
pedagogy. But traditional textbook-driven curricula seldom support this shift
effectively. There are some promising text materials on the market today that help
educators do a better job of teaching for deeper, conceptual understanding; but we
can't assume that teachers intuit the factual-conceptual-skills relationships in the
more concept-based materials. Curriculum materials can be powerful staff development tools if they clearly delineate and build relationships to help teachers
guide instruction between what students must know (factually), understand (conceptually), and be able to do (processes and skills). Learning experiences and
assessments need to reflect all three of these strands.

THINKING TEACHERS

Three-dimensional, concept-based teaching requires thinking teachers. A university professor told me when I began this work years ago that I was asking teachers to do something they weren't capable of doing—that it was "too hard for
them." Excuuuse me! Teachers across the nation and around the world embrace a
teaching model that values the intellect. It's true they have to make a mental shift
from the old, two-dimensional curriculum and instruction model, so it requires the
assimilation of new teaching paradigms and takes some practice. But once teachers internalize the basic principle of teaching to ideas with factual support, they
shift into high gear. It isn't long before teachers are using concept-based instruction to effectively challenge the minds of young people to even deeper levels.

When teachers are asked to make a significant change in their instruction, they
want to know why. And this is certainly a reasonable request. Chapters 1 and 2
present many reasons supporting a concept-based model of instruction. But there
is another reason for this requested change that has to do with motivation for learning.

Teachers in concept-based classrooms report that children are more highly engaged in learning—emotionally as well as intellectually. What would cause this greater degree of engagement?

Both concept- and non-concept-based classrooms provide interesting activities for students and have quality teachers. But there is a major difference. Concept-based classrooms structure the learning so that students are invited to process factual material through their personal, conceptual mind. This invitation comes in the form of a conceptual lens: "I'd like to invite you to think about our earth system in terms of *sustainability.*" The lens of *sustainability* invites students to think beyond the facts of our earth system and construct personal meaning. This invitation is highly motivating because we are intellectual beings who find satisfaction in using our minds well. The realization that engagement of an individual's conceptual mind increases his or her motivation for learning leads me to offer the following theory for consideration:

A Motivation Theory

It has been well documented that students begin school as eager learners, but motivation for learning declines as students reach the fourth grade and beyond. The preschool and primary grade curriculum is heavily concept based. These students are engaged in hands-on and minds-on activities to help them internalize the meaning of concepts: seasons, colors, animals, weather, family, and so on. Their minds are engaged in this synergistic interplay between the concrete and the abstract. But as the factual load increases in school and students are required to memorize increasing amounts of information, the conceptual mind is called upon less and less. I now believe that this declining call on the conceptual mind is a major reason for expressed problems:

a. Apparent apathy for learning in secondary schools

b. Substandard academic performance

c. Inability to retain important facts in long-term memory

Figure 5.1 illustrates this theory. Notice the inverse relationship between the increasing factual coverage and the decline in conceptual thinking.

Figure 5.2 illustrates that the problem can be rectified if we design curriculum and instruction so that the factual/conceptual relationship is maintained. This can only happen if we systematically design curriculum and instruction that engages students' conceptual minds as they work with factual knowledge.

INTRODUCING "BRAIN POWER" AND CONCEPTS TO STUDENTS

Concept-based instruction first requires that the teacher has made the mental shift from teaching to facts alone, to teaching to conceptual ideas using the facts as a supporting tool. Without this basic understanding of the relationship between facts

Figure 5.1

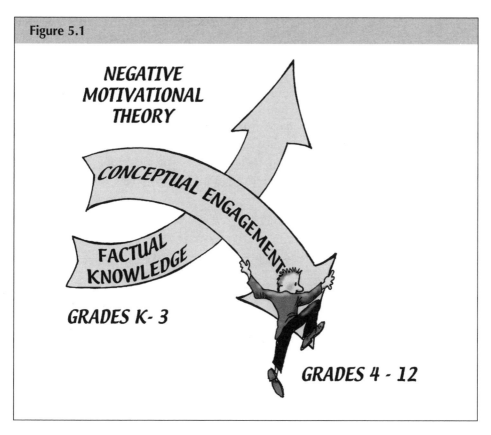

SOURCE: David Ford Cartoons, davidford@cablespeed.com. Used with permission.

Figure 5.2

SOURCE: David Ford Cartoons, davidford@cablespeed.com. Used with permission.

and conceptual ideas, the instructional monitor will only register intermittent blips of deeper intellectual engagement. Teachers want more than intermittent blips. We can provide concept-based materials and training to help them. Teachers who have internalized the concept-based shift in teaching pedagogy can consciously employ strategies to help their students understand that the brain operates at different levels of sophistication.

As soon as you feel your students can understand that our minds work "easier and harder" (early primary grades), or in "simple and more complex ways" (elementary grades), help them reflect on their own thinking processes. The following examples for different grade levels illustrate how you can make this point.

Early Primary

Teacher to students:

I am going to ask you to do two activities in cooperative groups. I want you to do the activities and then decide, as a group, which activity was *easier* work, and which activity was *harder* work for your brain. Be ready to discuss *why* one activity was harder.

Learning Experience A—"Sort the mixed group of colored chips (or blocks, etc.) into sets of like colors."

Learning Experience B—"Sort the mixed group of colored chips (or blocks, etc.) into sets of mixed colors and like colors. Make twice as many mixed color sets as like color sets."

After students understand from the follow-up discussion that Activity B required more thinking and asked the brain to work *harder,* then tell the students,

We can learn more when our brain is working harder. Some of our classroom learning experiences will ask your brain to work harder. I am going to give you an Activity Sheet for this week. I'd like you to put a check mark when we complete each activity telling whether your brain work was *easier* or *harder.* Then we will discuss why you think your brain had to work harder on some of the activities. (Our goal here is to have students be *conscious* of their brain working.)

1. (Learning Experience) ____easier   ___harder

2. . . .

Middle Grades

Teacher to students:

Our brains are amazing machines. Sometimes the thinking that we do is quite simple. For example, when you are recalling addition facts that you learned when you were in first grade, you don't have to think very hard.

But when you are given a story problem to solve that expects you to figure out which mathematics operations to use, your thinking is more complex—you have to think harder to solve the problem.

Teacher Note: At this time, you could do a simple presentation on the different parts of the brain (use a visual) and the job of the different parts. Tell the students that the prefrontal cortex is the place where more complex thinking occurs. (Students at this age would be very interested in a clear and succinct presentation on the brain and how it works.) After the presentation, challenge the students to work on using more of their brain's capacity.
Teacher to students:

How do we develop "brain power"? (Discuss.) This week, I want you to become aware of your thinking. I am going to give you a list of assignments that we will be doing this week. Next to the assignment, I want you to note which parts of the assignment were simpler and used less brain power, and which parts required more complex thinking and required greater brain power. At the end of the week, I will ask you to discuss your findings in a cooperative group. The question for your group will be, "How does a complex thinking task differ from a simple thinking task?" We'll then share your thoughts as a whole class.

Assignments	Parts	Simple	Complex
A.	a. _____	_____	_____
	b. _____	_____	_____
B. . . .			

If you feel that your students would be able to understand the Structure of Knowledge presented in Chapter 2, it would be a very useful tool to help them understand the difference between topics and facts, concepts, and big ideas (generalizations or principles) that transfer through time and across cultures and situations. The next example for secondary schools describes one way to introduce the Structure of Knowledge to students.

Secondary Schools

At the secondary school level, students are able to understand the relationships among elements in the Structure of Knowledge described in Chapter 2 (topics/facts, concepts, generalizations). They also are interested in the brain and how it works. It is helpful to discuss with students the brain's structure and how the brain operates to control physical, emotional, and cognitive functions. As with the elementary grade levels, secondary students need to become aware of the complexity of their thinking. So after a discussion and presentation on the brain and its functions, introduce the Structure of Knowledge:

Teacher to students:

We have been learning about the brain and how it functions. The brain learns new things through the experiences we have. At school, we participate in learning experiences using knowledge to develop our brains. But there are different kinds of knowledge. Today we're going to look at how knowledge is structured, and see how the different kinds of knowledge challenge our brains.

Teacher Note: At this point, put up a chart or PowerPoint slide showing the Structure of Knowledge from Chapter 2 with an example (topic, concepts, generalization) from the subject area you teach. Name the topic and read the concepts listed on the example. Do not read the generalization at this time. (Suggestion: To simplify learning for students, omit the "Principle" and "Theory" levels from the Structure of Knowledge.)

Teacher to students (ask guiding questions):

♦ "What is the difference between a topic and a concept?" (Students should deduce that a topic is specific, but a concept is broader.)
♦ "Which transfers to other situations—concepts or topics?"

When students understand that a concept transfers and that a topic is locked in time, place, or situation, put them into cooperative groups and ask them to brainstorm a list of topics and a list of concepts from the subject area under study. (Option: The teacher provides a mixed list of topics and concepts for student groups to categorize.) Cooperative groups partner and share their lists, giving feedback on the accuracy of the lists. Groups then post their lists around the room (teacher scans for accuracy). Once students are firm on topics/facts and concepts, introduce generalizations.

Teacher to students:

When you put two or more concepts into a sentence, you have written a generalization. (Read the generalization in your Structure of Knowledge example to the students.) How does a generalization differ from a fact? (You want them to realize that generalizations transfer just as concepts transfer, but facts are locked in time, place, or situation.)

Our brains are working at a lower level when we are recalling memorized facts. But when we think beyond the facts and identify important concepts—and then put those concepts together to make sentences of understanding that we can transfer to other situations—we are developing our brain power. We are making it easier to relate new information to our prior knowledge.

Teacher Note: Give all students a copy of the Structure of Knowledge with no topics, concepts, or generalizations filled in. Put students into cooperative work groups.

Teacher to students:

Now that you understand that you are thinking at more complex levels and developing your brain power, let's see if you can identify the concepts and generalizations for one of the topics we have worked with this year. (Give students a topic, or have them select a topic for their group.)

Work together to identify the concepts that are important for understanding your topic. Once you have your list of concepts, put them together into a sentence of important understanding based on the facts from your topic. Remember, your generalization can transfer to other situations, it will use a present tense verb, and it will not contain any proper nouns. To write your generalization, use the sentence starter, "We understand that. . . ."

Once students are more aware of their thinking processes, it is easier for the teacher to help them hold their thinking to "intellectual standards" (Paul & Elder, 2004a), which were discussed briefly in Chapter 1. I encourage teachers to expand their own understanding of intellectual standards and build reflective (metacognitive) work for students into classroom assignments. Helping students internalize when their thinking is clear, accurate, and insightful will not only increase their intellectual abilities but will also put them "in charge" of their own intelligence.

SAMPLE CONCEPT-BASED LESSONS

Elementary Grade Levels

Marianne Kroll, a master teacher featured in the ASCD video *Designing Integrated Units: A Concept-Based Approach*, shares a lesson she used for helping third grade students see how facts provide a "pattern of evidence." This evidence can be used to develop timeless, transferable big ideas (generalizations). Marianne explains, "The teacher keeps the generalization in mind as the lesson is planned, and constructs a chart using the concepts from the generalization as column headings" (see Figure 5.3).

Grade 3: Lesson on Natural Disasters

Enduring understanding: "Natural disasters affect daily lives and the economy of a community."

Guiding questions:
♦ "What is a natural disaster?"

Teacher Note: After discussing the idea of a natural disaster and having students name some different kinds of natural disasters, provide them with Internet or other appropriate reading material on Hurricane Katrina. Ask them to use sticky notes as they read, to mark places that tell about the impact of the hurricane on the daily lives or economy. Then use the following questions and fill out the Hurricane Katrina example on the chart with student responses. Leave the "Big Idea" column until each row has been filled in.

Figure 5.3 Natural Disaster Graphic Organizer

Natural Disaster	Impacts: Daily Living	Impacts: Economy	Big Idea
Hurricane Katrina (2005, southern U.S.)			
The tsunami in Southeast Asia (2004)			
Forest fires that threaten a community			

SOURCE: Marianne Kroll, Curriculum Consultant, Eleva, Wisconsin. Used with permission.

♦ How did Hurricane Katrina change the daily lives of people in communities like New Orleans?
♦ How did Hurricane Katrina affect the businesses and economy in New Orleans and other involved communities?

After taking the students through the Hurricane Katrina example, provide them with resources to complete the same process—in cooperative groups—of filling out the chart related to the 2005 tsunami and to forest fires. You could either specify a particular geographic location where forest fires threatened communities, such as in southern California, or you could have them generalize how forest fires would threaten the daily lives and economy of a community based on their work with the disasters just studied. It is important for the teacher to keep the relationship between the concepts in mind when constructing the chart.

When the groups have completed their charts, ask them to come up with a big idea in their work groups.

Teacher to students:

You have a lot of information on your charts about different natural disasters. Now think about the relationship among natural disasters, the daily lives of people, and the economy of a community. See if you can come up with a big idea *sentence* that would describe this relationship. Remember—you must be able to transfer your big idea sentence to fit any natural disaster in a community.

Have each group read their big idea to the class and ask, "Why do you say that?" (You want them to see that the information on the chart gave them a "pattern of factual evidence" to support their big idea.) You could post the big idea on a chart and tell students to be on the lookout for other examples of the big idea in the news. Students can add their examples to the chart as they find them. Another idea is to have students keep their own personal "Big Idea Booklet" with their own charts and student-designed graphics for a quick reference. As they come across an example of one of the big ideas in their booklet, they can add that example to their chart.

The purpose of the graphic organizer is to help students see that facts provide the support for concepts and transferable big ideas, and to help students realize that many different factual examples can support one big idea. But the chart also provides the teacher with concrete evidence that concept-based instruction is taking place.

After sharing the chart idea for this book, Marianne reflected on the importance of concept-based instruction:

> The emphasis on big ideas allows students to transfer what they learned from a unit of study to real life. Because thinking goes beyond the facts, students are able make, and actively look for, connections between different subjects, and real life. For example, students would often notice that an idea in social studies connected with something from a piece of literature.

Children enjoy the higher-level vocabulary associated with concepts, and they develop a deeper understanding of concepts and how to articulate their thoughts using conceptual terms. A teacher overheard two third grade boys discussing the book *Ramona and Her Father*, by Beverly Cleary, as they walked down the hall—"I can hardly wait to finish reading the book to find out how their perspectives affected the ending!" Through concept-based lessons, including in-depth discussions, students know that they are working toward something bigger than fact acquisition. Understanding becomes more important than memorizing.

Marianne and other concept-based teachers enjoy designing learning experiences that develop the conceptual thinking abilities of their students. Because teachers are using their own intellect in the design process, they are motivated in the planning and teaching. They are able to draw on the art as well as the science of teaching. In addition to the insights Marianne shared on the value of concept-based learning, there are some other benefits:

a. Children develop language abilities as they learn to articulate their thoughts.

b. Children learn the difference between opinions and ideas that are supported with evidence. (Concept-based teachers at all grade levels expect students to give factual support for their ideas.)

c. Children are motivated to learn because they are intellectually engaged at a more personal and challenging level.

Secondary Grade Levels

Following each sample lesson below, see if you can write a generalization that extrapolates the transferable understanding. Sample generalizations will be provided at the end of the section. After you have identified an enduring understanding for each selection, choose a particular type of learner (accelerated, delayed, English as a second language, etc.) and plan a differentiation strategy (see Chapter 4) to meet his or her learning needs for that lesson. These sample lessons were contributed by Rich Howe and Dennis Hillmyer, Trenton Public School District, Trenton, New Jersey.

1. **River Valley Civilizations.** Teacher to students: "In this lesson, you will learn about and respond to problems faced by people in the River Valley civilizations. You will learn how people living in farm villages were affected by problems such as flooding, insects, disease, or invaders."

Working in cooperative groups, have students choose a solution they think best solves the problem and prepare to justify their choice with two reasons. Emphasize to the groups that their plans may include only materials/tools that were available at the time, such as stones or shovels, and ingenuity.

Generalization: The students understand that . . .

_____.

Kind of Learner:

_____

Differentiation Strategy:

_____
_____.

2. **The Middle Ages.** "You are a newspaper editor doing a series of articles on life in the Middle Ages for the *National Courant.* Create four newspaper articles that each highlight one aspect of social, economic, and/or political change during that time. Then,

   a. create a political cartoon, drawing, or poem to capture how one of the changes is reflected in the society; and

   b. do the same (cartoon, drawing, or poem) to capture how a current social, economic, or political change is reflected in our society today.

"Write a paragraph responding to the question, 'How do your two products (cartoon, drawing, or poem for a and b) reflect cultural similarities and differences between the Middle Ages and today?'"

Generalization: The students understand that . . .

_____.

Kind of Learner:

_____.

Differentiation Strategy:

_____

_____.

3. **The Renaissance.** "Why was there a renaissance in Europe during the Age of Global Encounters? What were the effects of European expansion, trade, and colonialism? You are Owen or Abigail McCarthy—historical investigator seeking cause-and-effect relationships during the Age of Global Encounters. Create two graphic organizers tracing the causes and effects for two of the following topics:

    a. The Renaissance
    b. European explorations and colonial empires
    c. Slave trade
    d. Commercial revolution
    e. Scientific revolution and the Enlightenment

"In a paragraph at the bottom of your graphic organizer, explain how the cause-and-effect relationships you illustrated changed the society or societies involved."

Generalization: The students understand that . . .

_____.

Kind of Learner:

_____.

Differentiation Strategy:

_____

_____.

Possible generalizations for the sample lessons:

1. Cultures creatively respond to environmental and social problems using their available resources.

2. All cultures change socially, economically, and politically over time. Advances in technology, communication, and transportation lead to greater change and complexity in a society.

3. Key events in history can signal turning points that drastically alter the social, economic, and political directions of a society.

ADAPTING INSTRUCTIONAL MATERIALS

Educators who understand the significant relationship between the factual and conceptual levels for teaching and learning become more discerning when they look at curriculum materials. In the paragraphs that follow, we will "listen in" as a teacher, talking to a colleague, examines and shares the needed adaptations for different kinds of instructional material.

Textbooks. *Nice graphics. Appealing layout. Teacher-friendly. Uh-oh! There are fact-based objectives, but there are no enduring, conceptual understandings. If we decide on this textbook, we will need to identify the conceptual understandings for each chapter. We will also have to add conceptual questions to guide student thinking beyond the facts, and we'll have to adapt the instructional activities so they use factual knowledge to demonstrate the deeper conceptual understandings. Perhaps a better option would be to design our own concept-based instructional units—and use our textbook as one of several resources.*

Graphic Organizers. *Graphic organizers are such great tools for helping students process information. I have to adapt most graphic organizers, however, because they aren't requiring students to use their conceptual minds. I am pleased with my latest revision. Instead of having students give a traditional "book talk," sharing facts about the story and author, I had my students list key concepts from the story. Then I had them write three enduring ideas from the story using the key concepts they identified. I differentiated instruction by giving some students, who needed the support, two enduring ideas, and encouraged them to come up with a third idea. All students then found the factual supporting details from the book.* (See graphic organizer in Figure 5.4. For a completed example of Figure 5.4 and additional concept-based graphic organizers, see Resource D.)

Teaching Lessons. *I like this lesson on butterflies to support my Life Cycles Unit (Grade 2), but the lesson only covers facts about butterfly life cycles. I will need to write a few generalizations and questions to help my students understand that butterflies are only one example to illustrate the concept of life cycles. I also want them to understand the subconcepts related to the idea of life cycles. Adding these generalizations and questions will make this unit concept based and three-dimensional*:

1. All *living things* go through a *life cycle*.
   ♦ What is a life cycle?
   ♦ Why do living things go through life cycles?
   ♦ How many different kinds of living things can you name that go through life cycles? (List)

2. Some *life cycle changes* happen *quickly*; others occur slowly *over time*.
   ♦ Does the complete life cycle of a butterfly happen quickly—or more slowly over time? What about that of a human?
   ♦ Which life cycle change happens more quickly? . . . slowly?

   Birth

   Aging

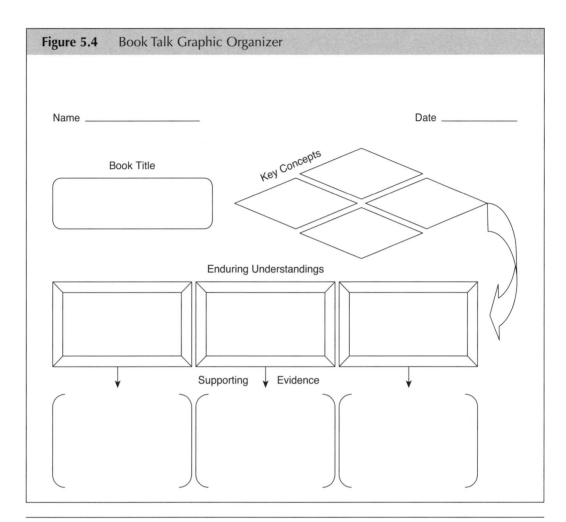

Figure 5.4   Book Talk Graphic Organizer

Name _____   Date _____

Book Title

Key Concepts

Enduring Understandings

Supporting   Evidence

3. *Changes* in a *life cycle* can be *observed* and *measured.*
   ♦ What characteristics can you observe in a life cycle?
   ♦ How could you measure the following characteristics: changes in height, changes in weight, number of physical changes?
   ♦ Why do scientists observe and measure changes in the life cycles of living things?

4. *Life cycles* can be *interrupted* by *natural disasters.*
   ♦ What kinds of natural disasters can interrupt the life cycles of living things?
   ♦ How might a flood interrupt the life cycles of plants? . . . animals?
   ♦ How can humans help prevent natural disasters and preserve life?
   ♦ (Higher-order question) Could an interruption in the life cycles of plants cause an interruption in the life cycles of some animals? How?

*Assessments. This performance task is two-dimensional—there is no require-
ment to demonstrate conceptual understanding. We can make it three-dimensional
quite easily, though, by deciding on, and writing, the essential, enduring understandings for the task, then picking up some of that language and building it into
the performance.*

Original Task: (two-dimensional)

Grade Level: Middle School

Unit Title: The Age of Global Encounters (1400–1700)

Performance Task:

You and a partner are modern-day adventurers determined to re-create the
voyages of two of the early explorers. Select two of the following explorers; use
the Internet and other sources to learn as much as possible about their major voyage. Record their reasons for exploring and their voyage experiences in a monthly
log entry for a six-month voyage.

(list of explorers)

Revised Task: (three-dimensional)

Grade Level: Middle School

Unit Title: The Age of Global Encounters (1400–1700)

Task contributed by Rich Howe and Dennis Hillmyer, Trenton Public School District,
Trenton, New Jersey.

Essential, Enduring Understandings:

♦ Geography and the search for specific resources influence exploration
patterns.
♦ Exploration for resources can lead to interactions with native peoples
and result in conflict.

You and a partner are modern-day adventurers determined to re-create the
voyages of two of the early explorers. Select two of the following explorers:

Sir Francis Drake	Christopher Columbus
Marco Polo	Ferdinand Magellan
Bartholomeu Dias	John Cabot
Vasco de Gama	Samuel de Champlain

Use the Internet and other sources to learn as much as possible about their major
voyages. Develop a voyage journal comparing each explorer on the following topics:

- Sailing route—create map
- The journey—monthly log entries
- Motivations to explore
- Description of the ship
- Discoveries in the new land
- Interactions with native peoples

Discuss in your journal entries *why the explorer chose the particular sailing route, and resulting interactions with the native people.* (Note the tie back to the essential, enduring understandings by picking up the language for the task.)

For your final journal entry, write two well-developed paragraphs discussing the following:

a. How underwater explorers of today determine their exploration routes
b. What environmental interactions and conflicts they need to consider

SUPPORTIVE BEST PRACTICES

Teachers sometimes feel that there are too many new innovations and strategies flying by, and that they are somehow not "with it" if they don't employ each new thing in their instruction. But there are some innovations that emerge out of the mix so grounded in quality research, or so steeped in commonsense education, that they resonate with most teachers and administrators and play out in classrooms around the world. These "best practices" enhance brain-based teaching and learning and reinforce the conceptual mind, so we will consider a few of them in this book.

Concept-Based Constructivism. Though the constructivist terminology remains popular today, the philosophical basis for the ideas has been around since the days of educators and philosophers such as Pestalozzi, Froebel, Herbart, Dewey, and James. As with most trends in education, the term *constructivist* has a continuum of interpretations that give students varying degrees of autonomy in selecting questions, issues, or topics to pursue. The current mandates of academic standards have reined in the purist constructivists who would prefer giving children free flight on the wings of knowledge. Jacqueline Grennon Brooks and Martin G. Brooks, in the updated version of their book *In Search of Understanding: The Case for Constructivist Classrooms* (1999), moderate the purist perspective through the presentation of four basic principles observed in constructivist classrooms:

- Teachers seek and value their students' points of view—students' perspectives are teachers' cues for ensuing lessons.
- Classroom activities challenge students' suppositions—meaningful classroom activities either support or contravene students' ideas, based on life experiences, about how their worlds work.
- Teachers pose problems of emerging relevance—constructivist teachers acknowledge the central role of the learner and structure classroom experiences that foster the creation of personal meaning.
- Teachers build lessons around primary concepts and big ideas.

This view of constructivist classrooms recognizes the critical role of the learner in constructing understanding, and the brain-based nature of quality designs for curriculum and instruction—designs that help students see parts (factual knowledge) in terms of wholes (concepts and big ideas) and that value the ability to transfer knowledge to other contexts.

Direct Instruction. It may seem paradoxical to discuss direct instruction as a brain-based "best practice"—especially following a discussion of constructivism. But quality instruction is at times direct, rather than inquiry based or constructivist. The research is strong in support of direct instruction, followed by guided practice, for learning situations like the following:

♦ Reading skill development
♦ Writing skill development
♦ Required memorized knowledge, such as multiplication tables, a piece of poetry, or a set of facts to be recalled
♦ Step-by-step procedures and skills, such as learning how to drive a car, constructing a cabinet, or rebuilding a car engine

At times like these, it is brain efficient and time efficient to use direct instruction. When skills are new and one has no prior experience to relate to, then direct teaching prevents confusion in the brain. But once the new skills are learned, then the generalization of these new skills is encouraged.

Differentiation. Carol Ann Tomlinson and all the educators who work to meet the unique needs of different kinds of learners remind us that children will never be "standardized." We can develop academic content standards to try to ensure a certain level of education for all our students; but as learners with independent minds, unique personalities, and a plethora of aptitudes and abilities, they will resist "extruder-type" education. So we do our best to meet different needs of many kinds (accelerated, delayed, linguistic, interest-wise, etc.) by adapting content, process, product, affect, and learning environment. It may seem too time-consuming to do the extra planning, but with a little practice, differentiation draws on the art of teaching. It is a creative process to think up ways to meet particular student needs. And the payoff for the student and teacher is well worth the effort in planning. Helping a child be successful as a learner builds his or her personal self-esteem and prevents the "I can't do it—I give up" syndrome.

There are other best practices that support concept-based learning. Practices such as cooperative learning, multiple intelligences, and inquiry-based learning are powerful ways to engage students in different ways of knowing and showing, and deep and extended dialogue. Dialogue is a powerful tool in the teachers' workbasket. It sharpens the minds of students as they play mental gymnastics with words and sentences crafting a question, stating an idea, or shaping a defense. All best practices give life to teaching and learning because they reach for individuals and draw them into the work with their minds and hearts.

SUMMARY

Concept-based instruction is an invitation to thinking teachers as well as thinking students. The art and science of teaching come together as teachers plan and design learning experiences that develop intelligence as well as a deeper understanding of content under study.

Teachers at the secondary school level complain that too many students lack motivation for learning. This chapter suggests the theory that student motivation may wane through the grades because the subtle shift to coverage of information through the grades leads to a decrease in the engagement of the conceptual mind; and the conceptual mind is the seat of one's personal intellect.

The conceptual mind is where one makes sense of information, finds the patterns and connections to create personal relevance, and puts knowledge together in new and creative ways. The conceptual mind is the uniquely personal intellect, and when our personal intellect is piqued and challenged, we are motivated to learn. When we are invited to bring our own thinking to a task, rather than simply memorize another person's thinking, we have the opportunity to use our mind well. And that opportunity correlates directly to our motivation for further learning.

This chapter suggests strategies for introducing students to the importance of concepts in developing brain power. If we are to develop critical, conceptual, reflective, and creative thinking abilities, then it helps to have strategies that encourage students to be consciously aware of how they are using their minds, and the kinds of activities that develop brain power.

Teachers benefit from looking at concept-based lessons and analyzing how they differ from traditional lessons. An elementary grade lesson shows one teacher's approach to concept-based instruction; and secondary teachers are invited to extrapolate the generalizations that are suggested in a set of learning experiences.

A concept-based teacher never looks at instructional materials in the same way after concept-based training. We "listen in" as two teachers discuss instructional materials from a concept-based perspective.

Finally, we take some time to consider just a few of the many best practices in teaching that support the concept-based direction. Constructivism (Brooks & Brooks, 1999), direct instruction, differentiation, cooperative learning, and multiple intelligences (Gardner, 1993) all have an important role in teaching for intellectual development and engaged learning.

Chapter 6 addresses an area that is critical to the improvement of curriculum and instruction—leadership. Chapter 6 bluntly states what professional educators believe. The chapter may create some discomfort.

EXTENDING THOUGHT

1. How does the author of this book correlate the engagement of a student's conceptual mind to his or her motivation for learning? Do you agree or disagree with this theory? Why or why not?

2. Why would a concept-based model for instruction conceivably provide more motivation for a teacher?

3. How does a concept-based lesson differ from a topic-based lesson? Do they both teach facts? (answer: yes)

4. How do constructivist learning, inquiry, and differentiation support concept-based teaching?

5. What kinds of criteria will you look for in examining curricular materials to make certain they support concept-based teaching?

Leadership Roles 6

The importance of quality educational leadership cannot be underestimated when shifting the paradigms of curriculum and instruction. Educational leadership starts with the superintendent and school board and moves through the central office staff to the site level—principals, assistants, teacher leaders, and teachers. Educational leadership is not a title. It is passion for a shared vision, the ability to mobilize people to solve problems and work toward goals, an intimate knowledge of all aspects of schools—curriculum, instruction, and child development—and most important, the inquisitive, continuous desire to learn as much as possible in order to do a better job.

DISTRICT LEADERSHIP

One of the best investments a school district can make is the hiring of a strong curriculum/instruction person as an assistant superintendent. The strength of an educational program depends on the quality of the personnel hired. With the laser-like focus on academic standards and achievement, it amazes me that so many school districts continue to use critical central office positions as musical chairs or, worse yet, "dumping grounds."

The superintendent position is critical for guiding the overall direction of a district. The best superintendents know the business from the ground up. They do not see themselves as only needing to deal with the "business" of schools. They are vitally concerned about the curricular and instructional program, because they know that the success of a school district depends on the quality of the curricular and instructional program for students. But the reality of the superintendent's office is that the day is consumed with public and policy issues. That is why it is critical that superintendents have assistant superintendents charged with overseeing the development of a quality curricular and instructional program. It is the

● 115

responsibility of the assistant superintendent to keep the superintendent and school board continually apprised of the direction and progress of curriculum and instruction for the district.

Why should the curriculum and instruction position be an assistant superintendent rather than a curriculum director? Because the position requires leadership beyond the school level to effect district change and progress in educational programs. A curriculum director can only "encourage" or "suggest" curricular and instructional changes to principals. They usually have parity with principals in the educational hierarchy. This means that when curriculum directors invite principals to staff development trainings on curriculum, principals may choose, or not choose, to participate. They may feel school matters are more pressing. And when curriculum directors set up curriculum writing workshops and need teachers to participate, principals may refuse to release them because they want them with the students. I can certainly understand their concern because it seems as if teachers are too often being called out of class for this or that workshop or training. But the reality is that without a quality curriculum to support quality instruction, students are shortchanged. The issue here is having a district focus on what is critical work and how to best use limited time to accomplish established goals—which reinforces the critical nature of quality curricular and instructional leadership at the district level.

Richard Elmore, in *School Reform From the Inside Out: Policy, Practice and Performance* (2004), reminds us that real reforms in teaching and learning take place in the classroom, and that if districtwide reform is the goal, there must be a commitment from district and school leadership to ensuring quality instruction in *every* classroom. This means providing such things as high-quality standards-based core curricula, professional development on effective instruction (including differentiation to meet the needs of various kinds of learners), accountability guidelines, and time for teachers and students to collaborate around student work.

We don't need district leaders who blitz staff with every new innovation of the day. We need thoughtful leaders who know how to work collaboratively with principals and teachers to build a solid curricular and instructional program for the district, with goals and time lines. Supporting initiatives, such as collaborative learning, are introduced at the appropriate places on the time line and are correlated to district educational goals, so that teachers and principals do not feel overwhelmed with too many innovations and directions occurring at the same time.

Because the assistant superintendent for curriculum and instruction is such an important position, it might be helpful to consider some criteria for hiring:

- A master's degree or higher in curriculum and instruction
- Successful classroom teaching experience (at least five years)
- Successful administrative experience (ideally at the principal level)
- Current knowledge of directions and research in curriculum and instruction (able to name, describe, and discuss current directions and a supporting research base)
- A vision for what quality instruction, curriculum, and professional development look like

- ♦ Demonstrated success in collaboratively leading curriculum-writing teams to produce quality curriculum documents
- ♦ Ability to communicate clearly and with confidence
- ♦ Past evidence of positive, collaborative leadership resulting in curricular and instructional change
- ♦ Ability to understand how to examine student work and make data-based decisions

It is the job of the assistant superintendent to see that the district curriculum is developed and implemented. The assistant superintendent should spend the majority of his or her time on this area and things connected to the area, such as required board reports on curriculum and instruction. If a superintendent needs extra support (to take care of the "other duties as assigned"), then a second assistant should be hired. If that is not possible, then a curriculum director, to support the work of the assistant for curriculum and instruction, is essential.

If a district has the resources, it is ideal to also have a staff development director working under the direction of the assistant superintendent for curriculum and instruction. There needs to be a close relationship between these two positions. The staff development director needs to direct the training to have new curricula implemented successfully and see that the support trainings (differentiation, collaborative learning, inquiry, etc.) are offered when appropriate in the overall educational plan.

Teachers and the public may decry the hiring of central office positions, but my experience traveling throughout the country is that the strongest districts have quality leadership in key central office positions. Ships need a strong rudder to maintain direction, and education can't afford to go bobbing along.

District Steps to a Concept-Based Model

District leaders want to know what steps can be taken to move toward a concept-based, three-dimensional model for curriculum and instruction. District leaders responsible for leading the concept-based direction must first understand, internalize, and support the goals to

- ♦ teach for *deep understanding* and the *transfer of knowledge* by using the facts as a tool to guide students to the deeper, conceptual understandings (generalizations, enduring understandings);
- ♦ develop a student's *conceptual brain schema* (brain structures) that facilitate information processing and patterning; and
- ♦ *motivate learners* by *engaging the personal intellect* in the learning process and by showing the *personal relevance* for content instruction.

The next section, "A District Plan," provides some reasonable steps to make the change from a traditional, two-dimensional model to the concept-based, three-dimensional curriculum and instruction model for schools.

A District Plan

1. Begin training district leaders (principals and assistant principals, curriculum/ staff development coordinators, lead teachers, etc.) on the *what* and *why* of concept-based curriculum and instruction to build a base of support and understanding.

2. Identify the key leaders responsible for the development, implementation, and evaluation of the curriculum. Work with them to clarify their responsibilities, tasks, and time lines.

3. Develop district core units (concept based) that *contextualize* the expectations of academic standards. (I would start with either social studies or science units because they would be the easiest.) District teams of teachers develop the units under qualified and trained curriculum leadership.

(Note: The language arts skills would be articulated and aligned to the academic standards through the grade levels. Concept-based core literature units could also be developed. In addition, leaders for the language arts area will want to read and consider the thoughts of Dr. Lois Lanning on text concepts and generalizations in Chapter 2.)

The mathematics curriculum would be articulated as skills through the grades—the more traditional format—but there needs to be another component added to the skills articulation for mathematics. The mathematics generalizations (conceptual understandings) need to be written next to, or above, the associated skills. Skill objectives are not enough if we want students to understand the conceptual base of mathematics that supports the skills. It is appropriate to develop concept-based *units* for mathematics at the secondary level (e.g., units on measurement or trigonometric functions).

4. Train all teachers on the *what, why,* and *how* of concept-based curriculum and instruction prior to the implementation of core units. Stress that the implementation of core units is meant to help teachers address the academic standards in a contextualized format (integrated into course and classroom curricula), and will provide guidance, as well as some flexibility, for carrying out the instruction. Create videotaped models of what quality instruction looks like based on the requirements of the curriculum and findings from research on quality teaching.

The nonnegotiables in the units are what students must understand (the enduring, essential understandings), know (the critical content—critical topics/facts), and be able to do (the required skills). Additionally, various assessments tied to these areas are nonnegotiable. Quality guiding questions and learning experiences provide models and suggestions in the units. Teachers are encouraged to develop additional activities and questions to teach to the enduring understandings and critical content. Teachers will need training on the difference between lower-level *activities* and stronger *performances* (discussed in Chapter 5).

5. Train building administrators and teacher leaders on the implementation of concept-based curriculum. Building administrators and lead teachers need to know how to observe, support, and guide teachers as they learn how to make the paradigm shift to a concept-based model.

6. Evaluate district report cards, teacher evaluation instruments, and so on, to see that they reflect conceptual as well as factual and skill-based components.

7. Develop teacher feedback systems to support the implementation of the curriculum. Receive feedback on such things as the following:

Need for further training on:

_____

Need for curriculum materials to support unit topics:

_____

Suggestions for unit revisions:

_____

BUILDING-BASED LEADERSHIP

Research studies and other writings clearly show that the success or failure of school initiatives is linked directly to the leadership ability of the principal (Cotton, 2003; Robbins & Alvey, 2004; Schlechty, 2005; Wagner et al., 2005). Principals are too often hired if they exhibit the requisite managerial skills, even if they have scant knowledge of (or interest in) curriculum and instruction. Yet the critical work of schools is curriculum and instruction for the quality education of students. Ask any teacher, "Is your principal a *manager* or an *instructional leader?*" They never fail to answer, and far too often the response is a chagrined, "manager." Teachers develop a dominant impression of their principal even though an excellent leader is both a strong instructional leader and a quality manager.

Chart 6.1 shares some commonly held perceptions that differentiate less-valued *managers* from more highly regarded *instructional leaders*.

The criteria for hiring a principal need to include an interest in the curricular and instructional program and, at the very least, the willingness to be a learner—with, and from, the teaching staff. The principal's job each day comes through the door in a seemingly endless parade of crises, issues, teachers, parents, and children. To be an instructional leader does require going above and beyond the swinging door. It is true that to "get to" curriculum and instruction, principals will have to use after-hour time to plan for the school needs and direction in these areas. They will have to value these areas enough to keep the staff focus and dialogue moving ahead. It would be very easy to let the swinging door define the principal's role—but the educational program will suffer without the strong support of the principal.

I believe that principals should come from a content teaching background (yes, an opinion) and see their role as an instructional leader as well as a quality manager. They need to be willing to read and explore curricular and instructional trends and research with staff as they work together to build a sound educational program for students. If there is an outstanding principal who comes from a non–content area teaching background, you can bet he or she is a learner who attends workshops with teachers and spends quality time in classrooms.

Chart 6.1 Managers and Instructional Leaders

Manager	Instructional Leader
Staff meetings are mainly for school business: upcoming events, supply orders, required paperwork for central office, etc.	Staff meetings are mainly focused on curriculum and instruction issues: discussing what is working and what is not, addressing issues that block teaching and learning such as absenteeism, and sharing what works in teaching (school business items appear in the weekly memo from the principal and take minimal discussion time in the staff meeting).
Looks for standards posted on the wall in classrooms or—worse yet—test scores posted on the wall.	Looks for essential/guiding questions posted on the wall (which are aligned to standards, factual content, and conceptual understandings) to engage student minds and interest.
Introduces a curriculum and instruction consultant in a school workshop on a major initiative and then ducks out to take care of school business. This conveys to teachers, "This workshop is not important for me."	Introduces a curriculum and instruction consultant for a school workshop on a major initiative and then participates with the teachers as a learner.
Is heard to say, "My teachers know best when it comes to teaching and learning. I just stay out of their way."	Is heard to say, "My teachers and I work together to build the strongest educational program possible for our students. It is my job to provide leadership and support for program planning, implementation, and evaluation. This must include a school schedule that allows time for collaboration: teacher/teacher and teacher/student."
Makes certain that the required evaluations of teachers are completed on time. (A reflection: How can one evaluate a teacher if one doesn't understand the curriculum and instruction?)	Dialogues with individual teachers on a regular basis to help them reflect on student work as well as celebrate their teaching and its impact on student learning.
Assumes that teachers and support staff are handling students with learning problems.	Knows the students and supports teachers in addressing the needs of specific students with learning problems.

Quality principals feel invested in the success of the district as well as the school. They are part of the district administrative team and work collaboratively with the superintendent and assistant superintendent, shaping their school identity and direction within the broader educational context of the district.

Figure 6.1

SOURCE: David Ford Cartoons, davidford@cablespeed.com. Used with permission.

I have met hundreds of outstanding principals over the years. And in some school districts they are found in almost every building. But I have also encountered the opposite—districts that seem to have misplaced the list of "Instructional Leader Questions" when they did their hiring.

The Center for American Progress, in conjunction with the Institute for America's Future, recently completed an 18-month study on United States schools. The report, titled "Getting Smarter, Becoming Fairer: A Progressive Education Agenda for a Stronger Nation," quotes Arthur Levine, the president of Columbia University, Teachers College: "The majority of the programs that prepare school leaders range in quality from inadequate to poor. . . . Many are engaged . . . in a counterproductive 'race to the bottom' in which they compete for students by lowering admission standards, watering down coursework, and offering faster and less demanding degrees" (2005, p. 52). I fear that one of the major problems we face in education is a dearth of quality leaders.

There is always a tension between district initiatives and school initiatives, just as there is a tension between the federal government and the state governments. Site-based management of schools used to be highly in vogue as districts cut back on central office staff and decentralized. With the implementation of state academic standards and their heavy expectations, however, districts could not afford to have a few shining stars. All schools needed to meet standards. The majority of school districts have reverted to central coordination of curriculum and instruction with core teams of teachers from the different schools writing the standards-aligned curricula for the district. I support this move for three primary reasons:

- ◆ All schools in a district do not have the leadership to guide the writing of quality curriculum documents.
- ◆ It is very costly in terms of time and money for each building to reinvent the curriculum-writing wheel. It is more efficient to have a core curriculum developed for a district by central teacher committees.
- ◆ Working as a well-articulated and cohesive *school system* is more effective and efficient than working as a *system of schools*.

If the core curricula are developed centrally, the building can focus their funding on staff development to improve instruction, or extended programming to meet the educational needs of students. New teachers, especially, need training and additional support to understand and implement the curricular program of the district. We are losing far too many new teachers in the first three years on the job.

Teachers are required to address core curricula aligned to academic standards. This does not hamper their teaching style. Teachers need some flexibility in *how* they deliver the curriculum. The instructional activities and guiding, or essential, questions should not be completely spelled out in a core curriculum. We don't want to give teachers such a detailed blueprint for teaching that it becomes their "script," and they are robbed of the opportunity to bring their own art, science, and mind to the planning. However, all teachers need, and want, a clear set of curricular expectations (know, understand, able to do) in this high-stakes educational environment. They also want and need opportunities to observe and discuss high-quality role models for effective instruction.

Principal's Role: Supporting Concept-Based Curriculum and Instruction

Dr. Leanna Isaacson, long-time principal, writer, and professor for Stetson University in Florida, worked with me to develop a set of suggestions to help principals facilitate the smooth implementation of a concept-based curricular and instructional program. We share these as ideas to add to your own repertoire of strategies.

1. Set a community-of-learners climate.

2. Listen to what teachers have to say about their needs in implementing the curriculum (time, support materials, etc.).

3. Allocate and direct funds to support implementation needs.

4. Verbally, and by action, express support for the curriculum.

5. Brainstorm and discuss with teachers what the concept-based classroom will look like.

6. Identify staff members and/or central office coordinators who can assist you and your teachers with a smooth implementation . . . and with ongoing

training. Plan one-, three-, and five-year benchmarks for teacher progress in concept-based curriculum and instruction. Require teachers to address these benchmarks in their professional development plans.

7. Plan ways for teachers to support each other in understanding and implementing the curriculum model:

   ♦ Encourage book studies
   ♦ Focus staff development based on individual and group needs
   ♦ Provide additional training and peer support for new teachers
   ♦ At the elementary level,
     • consider arranging sections of the media center by unit themes to support and supplement classroom resources and instruction on units;
     • provide central or grade-level storage of unit materials (in tubs, or some other manner) so that resources can be easily accessed by teachers;
     • develop a staggered plan for using the social studies and science units (in most cases, units do not have to be taught in sequence); and
     • discuss ways to efficiently share the unit resources and inventory unit components after each use. Note: This is often done by assigning a person at each grade to see that each teacher keeps the inventory up-to-date after each use. It is also helpful to have the entire school inventory on a database and/or media retrieval system.

8. Allow time for grade-level/department/team meetings in the building to reflect on implementation successes and "opportunities." These sessions can be facilitated by the principal, assistant principal, and/or teacher leaders. Teachers will want to bring examples of student work to show evidence of challenges and successes. Encourage the following:

   ♦ When sharing successful instructional strategies, comments, and questions
     • consider having teachers keep a reflection journal during implementation to
       a. note successful strategies to help students bridge from facts to enduring understandings;
       b. make notes for revisions on what is working and not working within the unit; and
       c. add guiding questions, instructional activities, or additional enduring understandings that they may develop to personalize their curriculum.

   ♦ Reflective problem solving to address issues related to the implementation, the curriculum, and/or the changes in instruction
   ♦ Collaboration on instruction and resources for special needs students such as learning disabled, ESL, and accelerated learners
   ♦ Peer coaching, including demonstration teaching, observations, and coaching (the principal needs to see that classes are covered)

9. Support implementation by asking teachers questions about their lesson or unit in pre- or postconferences:
   ♦ What concepts or generalizations are you working on in this lesson?
   ♦ What strategies are you finding helpful to guide students' thinking and understanding to the deeper, conceptual level?
   ♦ How well are your students understanding the big ideas?
   ♦ What evidence are you seeing and/or gathering?
   ♦ In what areas, such as unit components or instruction, do you need more help (e.g., peer support, extra inservice, coaching from a district trainer).

10. Provide weekly bulletins to support teachers for their achievements and also specify a focus for classroom visits the following week: "This week I will be looking forward to seeing the strategies you are using to help students bridge from facts to concepts and enduring understandings." During another week, "This week I would like to see how you are using factual, conceptual, and provocative (debate) questions to help students reach the big idea (generalization)."

11. Inform the community.
    ♦ With teachers, brainstorm ways to inform parents (over time) of the curricular and instructional direction. Do this step when you are confident that you can explain the direction and purpose clearly and confidently.
      • Have curriculum nights
      • Distribute newsletters (teacher and school)
    ♦ Tell the community what students are going to be learning; use a common vocabulary when talking about the curriculum and instruction. For example, use the words *concepts*, *conceptual lens* (for the unit), *unit title*, *enduring understandings*, *key facts*, *skills*, and so on.
    ♦ Let parents know that the curriculum is aligned with national and state standards.
    ♦ Optional: Share with parents some of the rationale of concept-based curriculum and instruction by referring to the Structure of Knowledge using specific examples from a unit for the different levels: topic and facts, concepts, and enduring understandings (generalizations). Stress that the curriculum is teaching students how to use facts to understand critical concepts and ideas that they can transfer to thinking about our world today.

Classroom Observations

Teachers should receive a set of the observation notes for concept-based instruction (see Figure 6.2) in their staff development training. The staff development program is responsible for ensuring that teachers understand these criteria and what they look like in practice. When making a curriculum and instruction change of the magnitude of concept based, it is critical that teachers receive

Figure 6.2 Observation Notes for Concept-Based Lessons

Lesson Focus:

◆ *Clear focus and link between content and concept(s) being explored*
◆ *Concept(s) for lesson apparent to observer*
◆ *Teacher develops the lesson to logically and inductively guide students to the enduring, essential understanding*
◆ *Teacher demonstrates a clear understanding of the relationship between facts, concepts, and transferable enduring understandings, and reflects the goal of teaching for deep understanding and the transfer of knowledge*

Instructional Strategies/Tools:

◆ *Teacher checks for prior knowledge of concept(s) and content for the lesson*
◆ New skills taught directly, not assumed
◆ Use of varied grouping strategies to achieve specific purposes: cooperative, paired, whole group, individual
◆ Use of multiple intelligences
◆ Differentiated instruction to meet the varied needs of diverse learners
◆ *Use of tools such as graphic organizers to help students process information—at the factual and conceptual level, and to relate the two levels*

Learning Experiences:

◆ Experiences have students apply previously learned skills
◆ Experiences reflect diverse needs of learners through "differentiation"
◆ *Experiences address what students must understand, know, and do (e.g., understanding generalization, know content, demonstrate skills)*
◆ Experiences are engaging learning experiences that accomplish a variety of goals:

   a. *Guide students to think conceptually using facts as a tool*
   b. *Guide students to see patterns and connections in knowledge*
   c. *Guide students to transfer skills and knowledge*

Guiding Questions:

◆ *Guiding questions are posted for the lesson.*
◆ *Questions reflect conceptual (transferable) as well as factual levels—perhaps use a philosophical (debate) question.*
◆ *Questions follow a logical path to guide students' thinking through the facts to the enduring understanding.*
◆ *Questions probe student thinking and encourage elaboration.*
◆ *Teacher asks students to support their understandings with evidence (experience, knowledge, or textual).*
◆ *Questions are linked to learning experiences and serve as a bridge between the factual content and the enduring conceptual understandings.*

Lesson Summary/Close:

◆ *Teacher assesses student understanding of the generalization* (enduring understanding) *in relation to the factual content either formally or informally.*
◆ *Teacher posts the enduring understanding.*

Notes:

◆ Italicized criteria are critical to concept-based instruction; other criteria are supportive of concept-based instruction.
◆ In addition to supporting a teacher's journey with concept-based instruction by helping him or her internalize the suggested teaching criteria, it is important to attend to what students are doing—and what they know and understand from the instruction. On classroom walk-throughs, kneel down and ask different students some questions:

   a. What are you working on?
   b. What are you trying to understand or learn?
   c. Is this easy or hard for you?
   d. Does this connect with anything you have learned about previously?

Students are living, breathing barometers for the impact of instruction and the energy of a learning environment.

supportive observations and feedback. The observation notes can be used by peer coaches, instructional specialists, or the principal to help teachers internalize the critical aspects of concept-based instruction.

For educators who are interested, Resource C has an example of a preobservation form for a teacher to fill out prior to a concept-based world history lesson for Grade 10, as well as an observation report to use in a postconference meeting with a teacher. This observation draws on many of the criteria in Figure 6.2 that are suggested for administrators and teacher leaders when making a requested classroom visit.

TEACHER LEADERS

Many schools have identified quality teachers as "instructional specialists," "lead teachers," or some other title to designate their role as support for the rest of the staff with curriculum and instruction issues (training, model teaching, etc.). At the secondary level, department heads often fill this role. This can be a positive step to give teachers more access to help with curricular and instructional issues and to extend leadership training.

Teacher leaders need staff development if they are to carry out extra responsibilities. They need training on such things as expectations for their position, curricula to be implemented, and effective staff development training. The identification of lead teachers does not absolve the principal of all instructional leadership responsibilities, however.

A chief executive officer needs to set the overall direction of a company. The principal is the CEO charged with the responsibility for the direction of a school. But the principal is not dealing with a lifeless, industrial product. To graduate successful students and citizens, the principal must be concerned with all the supporting elements: the curriculum, instruction, teachers, teacher leaders, school climate, and personalized attention to student and staff needs.

TEACHER TRAINING INSTITUTIONS

We can't leave this chapter without discussing the role of teacher training institutions. It has been encouraging to encounter new teachers in my workshops who are aware of and have received training from their colleges or universities on the latest trends and research in education. We still have much work to do, however. There seems to be a variety of obstacles to the upgrading of teacher training programs. One is that too many professors are working from traditional approaches to teacher education. They cling to outdated lesson plans.

Another problem is that professors are typically rewarded more for publishing research, rather than for working in partnership with schools. Their pay (as for all teachers) is poor, and they are given little funding to attend education conferences, so they more often attend conferences where they read their research papers. It would be much more valuable for student achievement if they attended general educational conferences where they could hear from, and interact with, teachers and professional educators from the field. Professors need to hear what is really taking place in the rapidly changing world of elementary and secondary education. We need to celebrate those many professors from teacher education who are keeping up with the latest research, issues, and directions in education.

Teacher training institutions vary greatly in their preparation of teachers. Many teachers feel their training was too basic—"How to write a unit or lesson plan with objectives," "What you need to know about teaching science, social studies, mathematics, etc.—'methods courses.'" And everyone learns about the history of education and the curricular theorists. But the complexity of teaching and learning today requires preservice and inservice programs that go beyond old methods and survey knowledge.

All teachers need to understand how knowledge is structured, the components of that structure, and the relationship to quality teaching.

Teachers must have practice in designing units and lessons that create a synergy between factual and conceptual thinking, and then have practice in three-dimensional instruction. In the last few years, I have seen more colleges and universities moving their teacher training toward this concept-based model. But the overall pace has the appearance of a seeping inkblot.

SUMMARY

This book ends where institutional change begins—with quality leadership. Moving from a traditional, two-dimensional curriculum and instruction model to a three-dimensional, concept-based model requires staff development training for all teachers and administrators, the adaptation of written curriculum to facilitate concept-based instruction, and the development of short- and long-range plans for achieving the goals.

The section on district leadership provides a plan for moving toward a concept-based model for curriculum and instruction, and the case is made to support the critical position of assistant superintendent for curriculum and instruction. It cannot be stated enough times—this vital position needs to be protected from a laundry list of duties. The focus has to be on leading the design, improvement, and assessment of the curricular and instructional programs for students. This is more than a full-time job.

A section on building leadership encourages school districts to hire principals who have the interest and teaching background to be instructional leaders for their schools. Principals who see themselves as managers, and leave all curriculum and instruction issues to teachers, leave a leadership void in the heart and soul of teaching and learning. And the teachers feel the void. At the secondary school level and in many elementary schools, teacher leaders can provide strong support, and these people are an asset to any school. But principals should never assume that these people relieve them of the responsibility for instructional leadership. Teacher leaders can help carry out a vision, but teachers will look to the principal for the final direction.

Leadership in all businesses is more difficult today because of the complexity of living in a global world. Education has also become more complex. I do not want to sound overly harsh in my portrayal of school leadership, but increased demand for accountability means that each job has a critical role in contributing to successful education. We now have a strong research base on child development and learning. Our challenge continues to be finding leaders who can translate this research into practice.

Hats off to the many thousands of educational leaders who make the difficult decisions each day, who work to improve their skills at collaborating and problem solving, and who are as interested in the curriculum and instruction for students as they are in the students themselves; most of all—hats in the air to the educational leaders who will always be learners themselves and who model this attribute for teachers and students every day.

EXTENDING THOUGHT

1. Why is it important for a school district to hire an assistant superintendent charged with the area of curriculum and instruction?

2. What relationship and responsibilities should exist between the assistant superintendent for curriculum and instruction and building principals when it comes to district-mandated curriculum—development, implementation, and evaluation?

3. How would you describe a principal that teachers see as a strong instructional leader?

4. Why is it important that schools have strong instructional leadership in addition to quality management?

5. What kinds of knowledge, skills, and abilities are attributed to strong teacher leaders?

6. What is your vision of a high-quality teacher training program—both preservice and inservice?

Resource A

*Concept-Based Curriculum
Glossary of Terms*

Concept: A mental construct that frames a set of examples sharing common attributes. Concepts are timeless, universal, abstract, and broad. Examples: cycles, diversity, interdependence.

Conceptual Lens: A macroconcept that helps learners integrate their thinking in a unit of study. The conceptual lens serves as a focus and a bridge between the factual and conceptual levels of knowledge and understanding. The macroconcept creates a mental synergy so that learners link new knowledge to prior knowledge and see patterns and connections between facts and transferable understandings.

Conceptual Theme: A unit title that includes a concept. Example: "*Systems* of the Human Body." A *topical theme* would not include a concept. Example: "The Human Body."

Conceptual Transfer of Knowledge: The application of concepts or universal generalizations across time, cultures, or situations.

Generalizations: Two or more concepts stated as a relationship. Also known as *essential understandings*, *enduring understandings*, or *big ideas*. Generalizations are conceptual understandings that transfer to other situations—through time and across cultures. They reflect the deeper understandings associated with specific factual content.

Integrated Thinking: The "meta-analysis" of factual information. When thinking is integrated, students see patterns and connections between the facts and related ideas that transfer through time, across cultures, and/or across situations. A conceptual lens, or conceptual question, facilitates integrated thinking.

Intellectual Character: Patterns of behavior, thinking, and interaction that are shaped and exhibited over time, and supported by "intellectual dispositions"—such as open-mindedness, curiosity, and skepticism (Ritchart, 2002, pp. 9–29).

Intellectual Standards: A set of traits, such as accuracy, clarity, depth, breadth, and relevance, which can be used to assess the quality of one's own or another's thinking.

Intellectual Synergy: A cognitive interplay between the factual and conceptual levels of thinking leading to deeper understanding and increased motivation for learning.

Interdisciplinary Curriculum: A variety of disciplines sharing a conceptual lens or focus for a topic of study. Thinking becomes *integrated*.

Intradisciplinary Curriculum: A single discipline study with a conceptual lens providing focus for a topic. Thinking becomes integrated.

Macroconcepts: The broadest, most abstract concepts. Often used as conceptual lenses to develop *breadth* of knowledge in inter- and intradisciplinary contexts. Examples: interdependence, change, systems.

Metacognition: Reflective thinking. Being able to analyze one's own thinking in terms of intellectual standards.

Micro- or subconcepts: The more specific concepts in a discipline. Students internalize these concepts, and their expanding relationships through the grade levels, to develop disciplinary *depth*. Examples: organism, character, proportion, migration.

Resource B

Curriculum Document Preface

The material in this Resource is offered to school districts to be used as a preface for district-developed, concept-based curriculum documents. It can be adapted to fit the particular district profile and needs.

CONCEPT-BASED CURRICULUM AND INSTRUCTION

The length of the school day and school year has not changed over time, but the world is changing dramatically. Global economics, politics, and social interactions and issues, along with advancing technologies, require more of citizens than surface knowledge and skills. The pressure on schools to help students think and perform at higher levels has never been greater.

The _____ School District has studied the research on learning and the brain, and has chosen a curriculum and instruction path that teaches standards-based facts and skills in relationship to the concepts and principles/generalizations of the disciplines. This concept-based model is not a faddish swing of the educational pendulum. It is a research-supported design based on the inherent structure of knowledge (see Figure 1).

There is an inherent relationship among *topics/facts*, *concepts*, *principles/generalizations* (essential, enduring understandings), and *theories*. Traditional curriculum designs focus on teaching topics and facts and make an assumption that students will understand the key concepts and principles of the discipline. Teachers intuitively teach to the concepts and principles/generalizations, but curriculum designs too often do not clearly articulate the concepts and principles to support the teachers' efforts.

Curriculum committees in the _____ School District have identified what students should *know* (factual content), *understand* (enduring, transferable, conceptual ideas), and *be able to do* (processes and skills). Curriculum committees have written the deeper conceptual understandings, in addition to clear statements

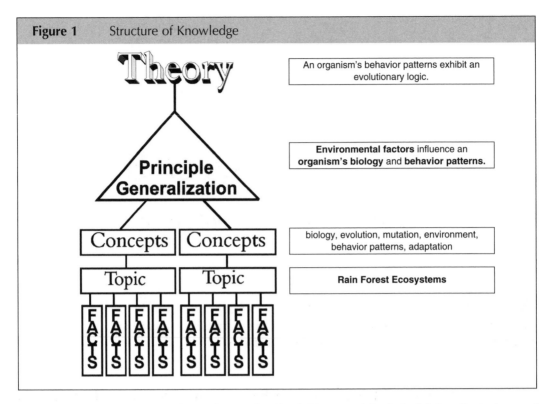

Figure 1 Structure of Knowledge

SOURCE: © 1995 H. Lynn Erickson, *Stirring the Head, Heart, and Soul: Redefining Curriculum and Instruction*. Thousand Oaks, CA: Corwin Press, Inc.

of factual knowledge and skills. This was not easy work, and the committees welcome thoughtful reflections and suggestions from all teachers and administrators as the work is refined.

Our school district believes that teachers need clear expectations on what their students must know, understand, and be able to do. Therefore, the district curriculum provides these expectations. They are correlated to the state academic standards. We believe that teachers do not need to be told which *verbs* to use (*define*, *list*, *explain*, etc.) to help students achieve knowledge and understanding. The art and science of teaching give teachers the prerogative in determining how best to engage their students. Teachers will want to draw from a wide variety of learning and performance modes. It is critical, however, that teachers design instruction and student performances that draw on the skills/processes of the disciplines. This means that teachers internalize the required skill sets of each discipline for their grade level or course.

It is important to help students develop the processes and skills of disciplinary ways of knowing and doing. Mathematicians, scientists, historians, and writers employ different tools, techniques, and perspectives to solve problems and understand the world. That is their strength. There are times in class when we will work within disciplines to strengthen disciplinary ways of knowing and doing, and there are times when we will pursue problems or issues through interdisciplinary perspectives.

The job of teachers in a concept-based model is to consciously guide students to a deep understanding of the concepts and principles/generalizations that structure a discipline. This is a paradigm shift from traditional instruction models. Instead of teaching to the facts only, the goal is to use the facts as a tool to help students achieve a deeper understanding of the transferable concepts and principles of the discipline. Certainly the critical factual knowledge is an essential goal, but it is not enough.

There are many reasons for teaching beyond the facts to the conceptual level of understanding:

♦ The fact base is expanding exponentially. A concept-based model develops a conceptual schema in the brain as a child moves through school. This conceptual schema allows students to pattern and sort information in the brain; make connections between facts and transferable, conceptual understandings; and relate new knowledge to prior knowledge.

♦ When students process factual information using a *conceptual lens,* or use factual information to support their deeper understanding of *big ideas* (generalizations), they

♦ retain the factual information longer because they have had to process knowledge on two cognitive levels;
♦ are more engaged emotionally and intellectually because they see personal relevance as they integrate new information with what they already understand; and
♦ think at higher levels because they must support conceptual understandings with factual content and experience.

Concept-based curriculum supports an idea-centered instructional model. We invite feedback and suggestions for refinement on the work to date. All suggestions will be considered as the curriculum and instruction program continues to evolve.

SAMPLE RESEARCH/SUPPORT BASE

Anderson, L. W., & Krathwohl, D. R. (Eds.). (2001). *A taxonomy for learning, teaching, and assessing: A revision of Bloom's taxonomy of educational objectives.* New York: Addison-Wesley Longman.

Barell, J. (1991). *Teaching for thoughtfulness.* White Plains, NY: Longman.

Bransford, J. D., Brown, A. L., & Cocking, R. R. (Eds.). (2000). *How people learn: Brain, mind, experience and school* (Expanded ed.). Committee on Developments in the Science of Learning and Committee on Learning Research and Educational Practice,

Commission on Behavioral and Social Sciences and Education, National Research Council. Washington, DC: National Academies Press.

Brooks, J. G., & Brooks, M. G. (1999). *In search of understanding: The case for constructivist classrooms* (Rev. ed.). Alexandria, VA: Association for Supervision and Curriculum Development.

Erickson, H. L. (2001). *Stirring the head, heart, and soul: Redefining curriculum and instruction* (2nd ed.). Thousand Oaks, CA: Corwin Press.

Erickson, H. L. (2002). *Concept-based curriculum and instruction: Teaching beyond the facts* (Rev. ed.). Thousand Oaks, CA: Corwin Press.

Gardner, H. (1999). *The disciplined mind: What all students should understand.* New York: Simon & Schuster.

Martinello, M. L., & Cook, G. E. (2000). *Interdisciplinary inquiry in teaching and learning* (2nd ed.). Upper Saddle River, NJ: Merrill.

Perkins, D. (1992). *Smart schools.* New York: Free Press.

Wiggins, G., & McTighe, J. (2005). *Understanding by design* (Exp. 2nd ed.). Alexandria, VA: Association for Supervision and Curriculum Development.

Wineburg, S., & Grossman, P. (Eds.). (2000). *Interdisciplinary curriculum: Challenges to implementation.* New York: Teachers College Press.

Resource C

Teacher Observations—Sample Forms

TEACHER FORM FOR REQUESTED OBSERVATION:
CONCEPT-BASED LESSON OVERVIEW

(Teacher completes prior to observation)

Teacher: <u>Jones</u>

Grade Level: <u>10</u>

School: _____

Date: October 2006

Unit Title: Prehistory: The Birth of Civilization to 1000 BCE

Lesson Title: Cultural Artifacts

Lesson Number: 4

Concept and/or Enduring, Essential Understanding:

Humans develop, and continually improve on, tools and other technologies to more efficiently meet their basic needs for food, clothing, and shelter.

Student Activities:

1. Research an artifact from an early civilization that was used to meet basic needs for food, clothing, or shelter.

2. Create a presentation (choices: PowerPoint, dramatic scenario, oral presentation, etc.) putting your artifact to use in the society it came from. Who is using it? What are they doing? What basic needs are they meeting? How did this artifact originate, and how did it evolve over time?

● 135

3. Share your presentation with the "Historical Society," an august body of your classmates. Respond to member questions.

Assessment:

Students will meet the standard criteria for a Presentation Scoring Guide (this would be attached):

♦ Presentation:

    Product—research knowledge, evidence of conceptual understanding (essential understanding) supported by research

    Process—oral presentation skills, drama skills, PowerPoint technology skills

Teacher Plan:

To help students realize the importance of artifacts in understanding early civilizations and how people developed tools to meet their basic needs, I will provide resources that describe artifacts of early civilizations. I will brainstorm with students a list of research questions that they would like to explore relating to the artifact/civilization they choose. I will provide process support in the form of a "Help Bureau" if students have questions or problems as they develop their presentation (PowerPoint tips, drama needs, etc.). I will differentiate the reading levels of the support material to meet the needs of different ability students, but I will expect all students to reach the essential understanding and concepts.

Guiding Questions:

The members of the Historical Society will have questions. I will ask some of the following questions after each presentation:

♦ Why are primitive societies more dependent on the resources in their environment?
♦ How do hunter-gatherer societies change when they gain tools and technology?
♦ Why did hunter-gatherer societies change to agrarian societies in the earliest civilizations?
♦ What inferences were you able to make about the people by researching the artifact?
♦ Is your artifact in evidence today in a different form? Why did it evolve?
♦ Why do humans continually change their tools and technologies?

Teacher Resources:

Teacher Notes/Comments (may be a request for the observer to note something in particular in the lesson, or for clarifying information prior to the observation):

For your visit, we will be making some of the presentations to the Historical Society. I would like you to key in on the student's understanding of how his or her artifact was used to meet basic needs, and how the artifact evolved. I would also like to have you consider the questions I ask each student. Are they helping the student understand the relationship between the development of the civilization and its artifacts?

OBSERVER FEEDBACK ON LESSON: FEEDBACK FORM FOR CONCEPT-BASED INSTRUCTION

(Observer completes during or after visit)

Teacher: Jones

Date: October 14, 2006

Lesson Title: Cultural Artifacts

1. Lesson opening/introduction:

   ♦ *Clear summary of the purpose and student work preparing for today's presentations*
   ♦ *Statement of the lesson concept—cultural artifacts and their importance in understanding early civilizations—set the context for the presentations.*

2. Student activities:

   ♦ *Research was thorough and related the artifact to the lifestyle and resources of the civilization.*
   ♦ *Your differentiation with reading materials and performance choices encouraged success for all children.*
   ♦ *Presentations reflected students' deep understanding that artifacts show how early civilizations met their basic needs.*
   ♦ *Presentations also demonstrated that students understand the concept of* artifact, *and how an artifact evolves over time.*

3. Clarity of conceptual focus for lesson in relation to factual content (concept and/or essential understanding):

   The presentations were focused on the concept of artifact, and the teacher directions and questions inductively guided students to the essential understanding that humans develop and continually improve on tools and other technologies to more efficiently meet their basic needs for food, clothing, and shelter.

4. Strategies/tools for guiding student thinking through the facts to the essential understanding (e.g., graphic organizer, use of guiding questions, grouping format, different modalities [intelligences] addressed):

   Though this lesson was a performance based on earlier research, the directions for the student activities tie clearly to the essential understanding and concept.

5. Fusion of skills into student work:

Allowing students to select a medium (PowerPoint, drama, oral presentation, etc.) lets them use their preferred form of expression and encourages them to meet a variety of standards-based skills. The Scoring Guide for process work effectively addresses the skill standards.

6. Use of guiding questions (factual, conceptual, and essential [provocative] questions):

♦ Are questions asked in a logical "path" to guide student thinking?

Your questions were appropriate and logically "pathed" for each presentation.

♦ Do questions work through the facts to guide students to the essential understanding?

Your questions helped students make the connections from the facts to the essential understanding.

♦ Other observations

7. Lesson closure (Was the enduring, essential understanding tied to the supporting content in the close—and then posted?):

If you post the essential understanding on a chart at the close of the presentations and summarize the presentations in terms of the understanding, you will help reinforce the transferability of the idea. You could also ask, "Do we have artifacts today that show how we meet our basic needs? What might they be? How do you think people who find our artifacts a thousand years from now will characterize our society?"

8. Assessment (Are factual, conceptual, and skill levels assessed? How?):

The Scoring Guides accurately reflect your standard criteria for what students must know, understand, and be able to do.

Follow-Up Meeting:

Teacher Comments/ Perceptions:	Observer Comments/ Perceptions:
	Excellent job! I was impressed with clarity in instruction, and the way in which you guided the students to use their facts to understand the transferable knowledge.
	Your essential understanding is important for helping students understand the evolution of civilization in terms of meeting basic needs.
	The fact that you used differentiation strategies without sacrificing the expectations for knowledge and understanding shows your adherence to high standards for all students.

Resource D

Concept-Based Graphic Organizers

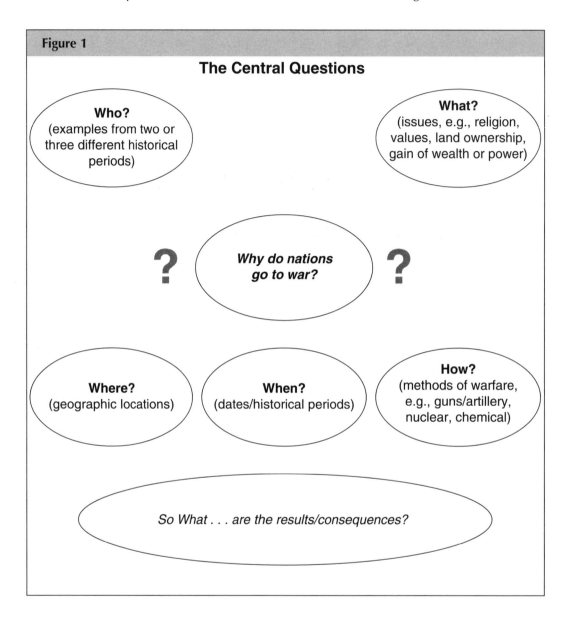

Figure 1

The Central Questions

Who?
(examples from two or three different historical periods)

What?
(issues, e.g., religion, values, land ownership, gain of wealth or power)

? **Why do nations go to war?** ?

Where?
(geographic locations)

When?
(dates/historical periods)

How?
(methods of warfare, e.g., guns/artillery, nuclear, chemical)

So What . . . are the results/consequences?

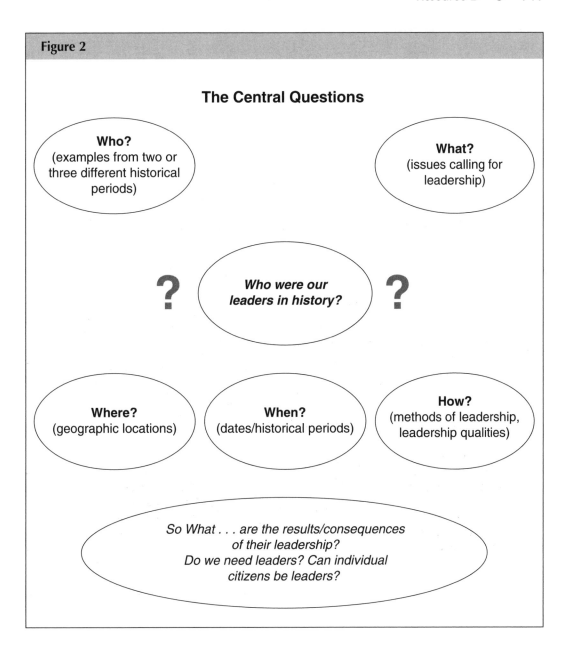

Figure 2

The Central Questions

Who?
(examples from two or three different historical periods)

What?
(issues calling for leadership)

? *Who were our leaders in history?* **?**

Where?
(geographic locations)

When?
(dates/historical periods)

How?
(methods of leadership, leadership qualities)

So What . . . are the results/consequences of their leadership?
Do we need leaders? Can individual citizens be leaders?

Figure 3

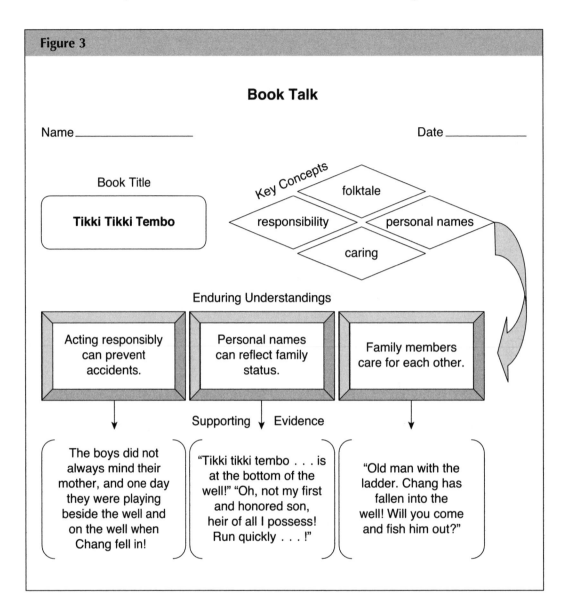

Book Talk

Name_____   Date_____

Book Title   Key Concepts

Tikki Tikki Tembo

folktale

responsibility   personal names

caring

Enduring Understandings

| Acting responsibly can prevent accidents. | Personal names can reflect family status. | Family members care for each other. |

Supporting ↓ Evidence

The boys did not always mind their mother, and one day they were playing beside the well and on the well when Chang fell in!

"Tikki tikki tembo . . . is at the bottom of the well!" "Oh, not my first and honored son, heir of all I possess! Run quickly . . . !"

"Old man with the ladder. Chang has fallen into the well! Will you come and fish him out?"

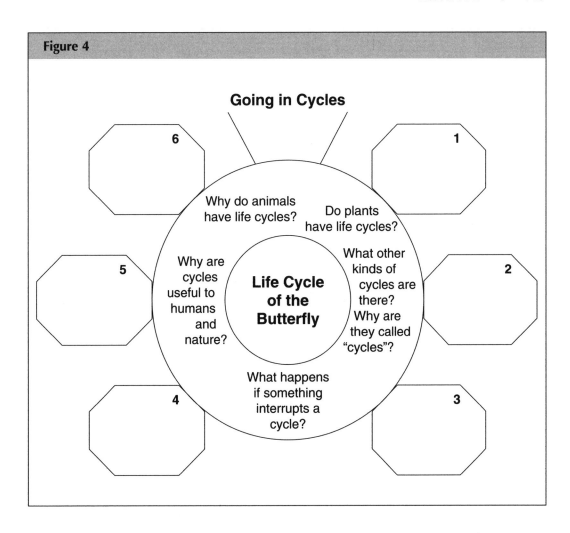

Figure 4

Figure 5

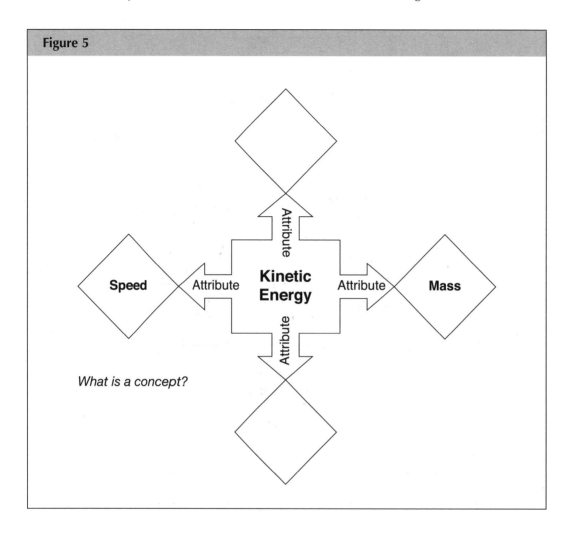

What is a concept?

Figure 6

Tracking the Facts

Subject Examples	*Items to compare*				
	Food	Housing	Clothing	Environment	Beliefs
Plains Indians					
Northwest Coast Indians					
Southwest Indians					

Research Topic **Native American Tribes**   Name _____   Date _____

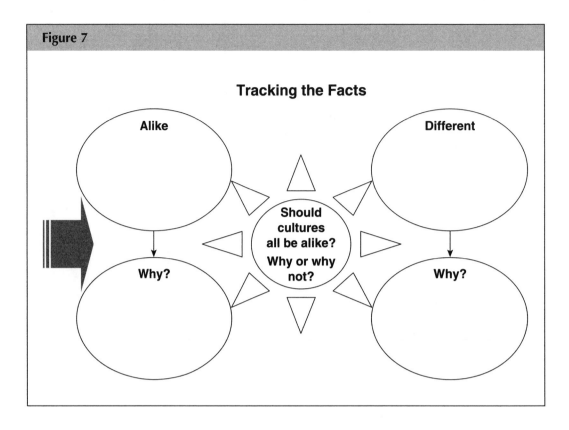

Figure 7

Tracking the Facts

Alike

Different

Should cultures all be alike? Why or why not?

Why?

Why?

Resource E1

Sample Unit and Lesson Planner

Figure 1

Unit Planner

Unit Title:_____

Conceptual Lens:_____

Unit Overview

Unit Title

Designer(s):_____

Grade Level:_____

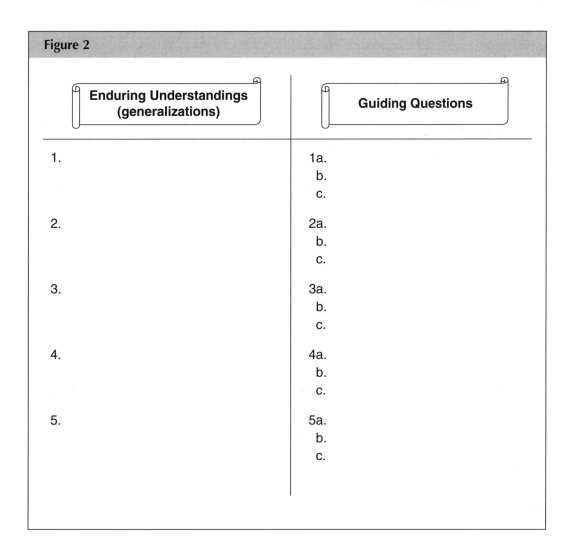

Figure 2

Enduring Understandings (generalizations)	Guiding Questions
1.	1a. b. c.
2.	2a. b. c.
3.	3a. b. c.
4.	4a. b. c.
5.	5a. b. c.

Figure 3				

AC = Assessment Code:

Q - Quizzes   P - Prompts
T - Tests   O - Observations
WS - Work Samples   D - Dialogues
SA - Student Self-Assessment

Critical Content and Skills:

Students will know (factual) . . .	AC			AC
1.		4.		
2.		5.		
3.		6.		

Key skills (transferable) . . .	AC			AC
1.		4.		
2.		5.		
3.		6.		

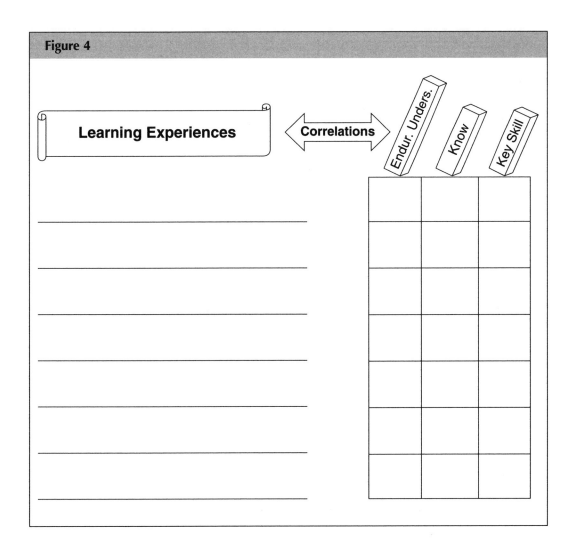

Figure 4

Learning Experiences ⟵⟶ Correlations Endur. Unders. Know Key Skill

Figure 5

Performance Task Planner

What: Investigate (topic) . . .

Why: In order to understand that (generalization) . . .

How: (performance idea to be developed into an engaging
      scenario on the following page)

Figure 6

Engaging Scenario

Figure 7

Task Criteria

(to be used for evaluation)

Figure 8

Scoring Guide

(For upper grades)

Possible Points or %

Self-Assessment

Teacher Assessment

Scoring Criteria

S
t
a
n
d
a
r
d

Scoring Key
A =
B =
C =
I =

100 _____ _____

NOTE: I = Incomplete

Figure 9

Scoring Guide   (For Early Elementary Grades)

4 Meets and exceeds standard criteria:
Examples:

(Check if met)

S t a n d a r d **3**

☐

☐

☐

☐

2 Meets 3/4 of the criteria in the standard

1 Non-scorable; does not yet approach standard

Figure 10

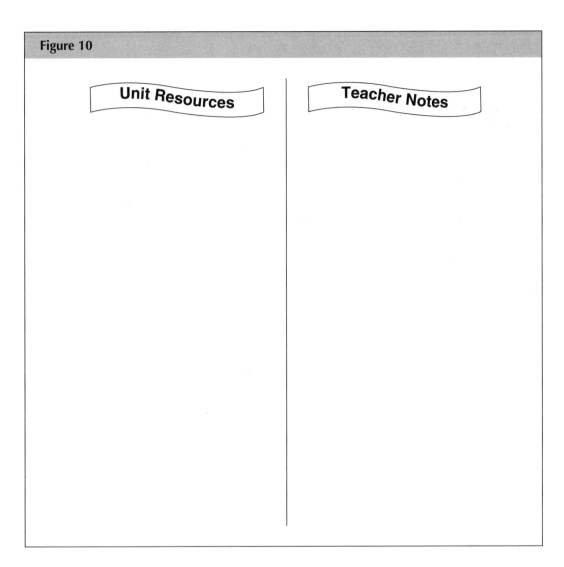

Unit Resources

Teacher Notes

Figure 11

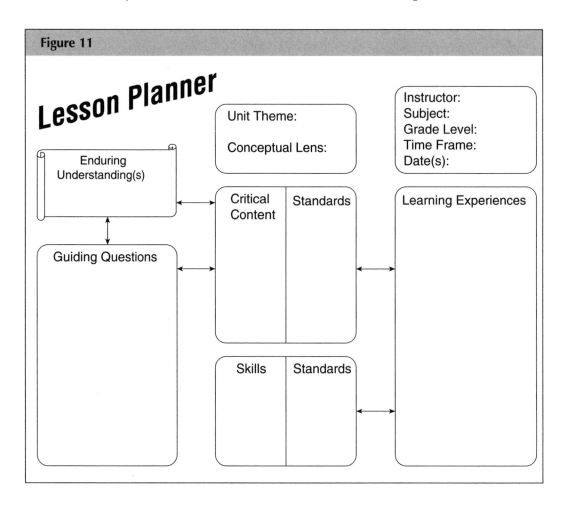

Figure 12

Lesson Planner

Instructor_____

Instructional Strategies	Differentiation Strategies	Assessment Strategies

Materials/Resources	Teacher Notes

Resource E2

Completed Unit and Lesson Planner

Figure 1

Conceptual Lens: Revolution

Middle School

History

6.5C1 ◆ Causes and results of the American Revolution
- political, ideological, religious, and economic origins of the Revolution
- reason for the win against superior British resources

6.6C1 ◆ *New Jersey's critical role in the American Revolution*
- *major battles*
- *viewpoints of Loyalists*
- *involvement of women and African Americans*

Economics

6.5C2 ◆ Revolutionary War debt
- response by states and the Continental Congress

6.5C2 ◆ Dispute over western lands
- issues and resolution

6.6C2 ◆ *Impact of the American Revolution on New Jersey economics*

(Unit title)

Revolution and the New Nation 1754–1820s

Geography

6.5C1 ◆ Interpretation of historical maps

6.6C2 ◆ Types of maps
- physical
- political
- topographic
- demographic

Government

6.5C1 ◆ Declaration of Independence
- fundamental contradictions between the ideals in the Declaration and the realities of chattel slavery

6.5C1 ◆ Treaty of Paris
- terms of agreement
- effect on U.S. relations with Native Americans and with European powers holding North American territories

6.9C3 ◆ Accomplishments and failures of the Continental Congress

6.2B1 ◆ The Constitutional Convention
- alternative plans considered by delegates and the major compromises agreed upon to gain approval of the Constitution

6.2B1 ◆ Bill of Rights
- arguments presented
- Madison's role in securing adoption

6.2B1 ◆ Development of the Supreme Court's power and its significance from 1789–1820
- John Marshall's Constitutional interpretations
- establishment of the Supreme Court

6.5C3 ◆ American two-party system
- opposing views on the main economic and foreign policy issues of the 1790s

◆ Influence of the French Revolution on American politics

6.6B1 ◆ *Origins, history, and recent applications of essential ideas embodied in the U.S. and New Jersey Constitutions*

Culture

6.5B2 ◆ Effects of the American Revolution on different social groups
- reasons for loyalty to the British by many white men and women, most African Americans, and Native Americans

6.5B2 ◆ arguments for new women's roles and 18th-century limits on women's aspirations
- *impact of American Revolution on NJ society*

6.6C2

6.9C3 - examples in which social institutions failed to function in a positive way:
  ♦ cruel and inhumane behavior
  ♦ cultural conflicts
  ♦ prejudice
  ♦ African slave trade
  ♦ Native Americans

SOURCE: Rich Howe & Dennis Hillmyer, Trenton Public Schools, Trenton, New Jersey. Used with permission.

Figure 2

Revolution and the New Nation: 1754–1820

Essential Understandings/Guiding Questions:

Government:

1. Nations may form alliances to further political and/or economic self-interests.
- Why do nations form alliances? - How do nations form alliances? - How do alliances affect political or economic self-interests? - Are all alliances beneficial? - Should nations form alliances? - In what way did the United States form an alliance in this period to further its political or economic self-interest?

2. Political revolutions are fought to gain freedoms from, or changes in, the controlling government.
- What is a revolution? - What is *freedom?* - Why do people want freedom? - How is a government affected by the social culture of a nation? - In what way did the American Revolution change the controlling government? - What does freedom entail? - What are the responsibilities of having freedom?

3. Democratic governments seek public support and use compromise to settle national policy debates.
- What is a democratic government?
- Why do governments need public support?
- What is compromise?
- How does compromise settle national policy?
- Why do governments need compromise?
- In what ways did the United States use compromise to extend democracy?
- Why do democratic societies create political parties?
- Why do these political parties differ in their beliefs and viewpoints?

(Continued)

Figure 2 (Continued)

Culture:

4. War can stimulate, depress, or decimate the economy of a region or nation.

- What is war? - Why do nations go to war? - Why do wars differ in their impact on an economy? - What effect did the American Revolution have on the economy in early America? - Are wars sometimes necessary? Under what circumstances?

5. Revolutions can change social, economic, and political relationships in a country.

- What is a revolution? - Why do revolutions occur? - Why do revolutions differ? - How does a revolution affect the economic life and social relationships of a country? - How did the American Revolution change the economic life and social relationships in early America? - How did the American Revolution lead to political conflict in early America? - Are all revolutions violent? Why or why not?

6. Cultural conflicts can lead to discrimination and prejudice.

- What is culture? - What is *cultural conflict*? - Why do cultures differ? - What is discrimination? - What is prejudice? - What is bias? - Why do different cultures compete for social supremacy even though it leads to conflict? - How did cultural conflicts affect the American Revolution?

Economics/Government:

7. Countries carry out political, military, and economic expansion to increase wealth, power, and prestige.

- Why do nations want to expand? - How do nations expand? - How do nations organize to carry out expansion activities? - Why do nations desire wealth, power, and prestige? - Why do these desires often result in the domination of other cultures? - In what ways did expansion affect the United States? - What were the United States expansion patterns during the American Revolutionary period? - What were the expansion boundaries between 1754 and 1820?

8. The desire of countries to satisfy their needs and wants can cause social and political conflict.

- What is the difference between a need and a want? - What kinds of needs and wants do countries have? - Why do countries have conflicts over needs and wants? - Why do needs and wants cause social and political unrest? - What things in politics and society did the United States use to satisfy its needs and wants? - How did the desires of other groups and the United States affect society and politics? - Should countries be allowed to invade other countries to meet their needs and wants?

9. Countries may control colonies for economic benefit.

- What is a colony? - What is the economic benefit of a colony? - How did the development of colonies change the economic and political growth of nations? - Should nations have colonies? - How did the 13 colonies differ from other colonies in the world in the Revolutionary period?

10. Subversive groups can resist a foreign influence.

- What is a subversive group? - How do subversive groups influence foreign cultures? - In what way did the 13 colonies use subversive groups to impact the British? - In what ways are heroes and terrorists the same and different? Who are the heroes and who are the terrorists?

11. Geography affects the way people satisfy their needs and wants.

- How can needs and wants cause conflict? - Why do needs and wants affect geography? - How can conflict over geography lead to the change of land boundaries?

12. Geography can establish the way a war is fought.

- How does geography affect how war is fought? - Why does geography affect war strategies?

Figure 5.3

Critical Content and Skills:

Students will know...

1. The background, major issues, events, and personalities (Washington, other founders) of the American Revolution, including the political and economic causes and consequences of the Revolution

2. The role New Jersey played in the American Revolution

3. The path of American territorial expansions and the settlement of the frontier

4. The early development of political parties, including the issues in the federalist–anti-federalist controversy

Key skills...

1. Use technology to access and present historical information.

2. Assess the validity of sources when accessing historical information.

3. Evaluate perspective and viewpoint in historical accounts.

4. Write a script of main ideas and supporting information to guide an oral presentation.

5. Create a storyboard for a presentation.

6. Develop a computer-based presentation to share historical information.

Figure 4

Suggested Learning Experiences ⟨ Correlations ⟩

Suggested Learning Experiences	Essen. Unders.	Know	Key Skill
A. Carry out a teacher-developed "Web Quest" to find historical information on the Internet.			1,2,3
B. Work with a partner to create a storyboard of your Web Quest findings. From the storyboard, create a Hypercard, Hyperstudio, KidPix, or PowerPoint presentation to share with your classmates.			5,6
C. What role did New Jersey play in the American Revolution? Create ten journal entries including the major battles, the viewpoints of the Loyalists, and the involvement of women and African Americans.	2,7,8, 10,16	1,2	3
D. Take the position of an anti-federalist or a federalist. Write a newspaper article for the *Colony Times* lobbying the public to support your position on the role of a federal government. Provide logical reasoning for your position.	3,5	4	3
E. Present an oral report on the anti-federalist/federalist debate. Describe the different perspectives and the attempts for compromise.	3,5	4	
F. Culminating Performance Task – American Revolution	2,5,7, 8,9,10	1	1,2,3, 4,5,6

Note: Correlate by number to unit components

Figure 5

Culminating Performance Task Planner—American Revolution

What: Investigate the American Revolution and the New Nation (1754–1820)

Why: In order to understand that political revolutions are fought to gain freedoms from, or changes in, the controlling government

How: (Engaging Scenario   Performance)

The students in Mrs. Wright's class are going to be learning about the American Revolution.
You are going to be "teacher for a day" and help her students understand that . . .
Political revolutions are fought to gain freedoms from, or changes in, the controlling government.

1. Using the teacher-developed Web Quest, research the causes, events, and key figures of the American Revolution (see Teacher Notes).

2. Create a Hypercard, Hyperstudio, KidPix, or PowerPoint presentation for Mrs. Wright's class to help them understand why the colonists wanted to be free of English rule.
   a. Develop a *storyboard* of your presentation—a paper-and-pencil sketch of the entire presentation, screen by screen. Sketch text, images, sound, motion, or interactivity that you wish to place on each screen. This is a quick sketch rather than beautiful artwork. Include major events and key figures.
   b. Create the presentation from your storyboard plan.
   c. End the presentation with a discussion question for your audience about *freedom* or *revolution*.

3. Develop a written script for your presentation.

4. Present to Mrs. Wright's class and end with your question.

Figure 6

Task Criteria for American Revolution Technology-Based Presentation
(to be used for evaluation)

Content:

♦ Hypercard, Hyperstudio, KidPix, or PowerPoint presentation reflects thorough and accurate research on the causes, major events, and key figures of the American Revolution.

♦ The concept of *freedom from oppression* is clearly portrayed as a major cause of the Revolution.

♦ The final discussion question on *freedom* or *revolution* provokes interest and deeper thinking in the audience.

Process:

♦ The Hypercard, Hyperstudio, KidPix, or PowerPoint presentation flows logically from the storyboard plan.

♦ Slides are easy to read and understand.

♦ Graphics, including animation, clip art, or pictures, enhance the message and are not "overdone."

Note: Use a district Oral Presentation Rubric to evaluate the presentation to Mrs. Wright's class.

Figure 7

Scoring Guide

		Possible Points or %	Self-Assessment	Teacher Assessment
	Scoring Criteria			
Standard	**Content:** Hypercard, Hyperstudio, KidPix, or PowerPoint presentation reflects thorough and accurate research on the causes, major events, and key figures of the American Revolution.	30		
	The concept of *freedom from oppression* is clearly portrayed as a major cause of the Revolution.	20		
	The final discussion question on *freedom or revolution* provokes interest and deeper thinking in the audience.	15		
	Process: The Hypercard, Hyperstudio, KidPix, or PowerPoint presentation flows logically from the storyboard plan.	15		
	Slides are easy to read and understand.	10		
	Graphics, including animation, clip art, or pictures, enhance the message and are not "overdone."	10		

Scoring Key   100   _____   _____

A = 90–100
B = 80–89
C = 70–79
I = Below 70

NOTE: I = Incomplete

Figure 8

Unit Resources

Approved textbooks;
supplementary materials;
the Internet

Teacher Notes

**Culminating Performance
Task – American Revolution**

1. Differentiation: You may choose to have
students work in teams to research and create
the presentation. Each student must be
assigned specific tasks. For example,
all students could do the Web Quest research
and plan the storyboard, and each could develop
one or more slides to go into the presentation.
Some students could write the script for the oral
presentation, and selected students could
present to the fifth grade classes using the
scripted talk along with the technology.

2. The teacher may choose to facilitate the final
question discussion or have the presenter
facilitate.

3. Web Quest—
To view Web Quest learning in social studies,
go to the Web Quest page,
http://webquest.sdsu.edu/webquest.html

Resource F

The Knowledge Domain and
Cognitive Processes

Figure 1

THE KNOWLEDGE DIMENSION
MAJOR TYPES AND SUBTYPES

EXAMPLES

A.	FACTUAL KNOWLEDGE—The basic elements students must know to be acquainted with a discipline or to solve problems in it
AA.	Knowledge of terminology	Technical vocabulary, musical symbols
AB.	Knowledge of specific details and elements	Major natural resources, reliable sources of information

B.	CONCEPTUAL KNOWLEDGE—Constructing meaning from instructional messages, including oral, written, and graphic communication
BA.	Knowledge of classifications and categories	Periods of geological time, forms of business ownership
BB.	Knowledge of principles and generalizations	Pythagorean theorem, law of supply and demand
BC.	Knowledge of theories, models, and structures	Theory of evolution, structure of Congress

C.	PROCEDURAL KNOWLEDGE—How to do something, methods of inquiry, and criteria for using skills, algorithms, techniques, and methods
CA.	Knowledge of subject-specific skills and algorithms	Skills used in painting with watercolors, whole number division algorithm
CB.	Knowledge of subject-specific techniques and methods	Interviewing techniques, scientific method
	Knowledge of criteria for determining when to use appropriate procedures	Criteria used to determine when to apply a procedure involving Newton's second law, criteria usedto judge the feasibility of using a particular method to estimate business costs

D.	METACOGNITIVE KNOWLEDGE—Knowledge of cognition in general as well as awareness and knowledge of one's own cognition
DA.	Strategic knowledge	Knowledge of outlining as a means of capturing the structure of a unit of subject matter in a textbook, knowledge of basic heuristics
DB.	Knowledge about cognitive tasks, including appropriate contextual and conditional knowledge	Knowledge of the types of tests particular teachers administer, knowledge of the cognitive demands of different tasks
DC.	Self-knowledge	Knowledge that critiquing essays is a personal strength whereas writing essays is a personal weakness, awareness of one's own knowledge level

SOURCE: From Lorin W. Anderson and David R. Krathwohl, *A Taxonomy for Learning, Teaching, and Assessing: A Revision of Bloom's Taxonomy of Educational Objectives*. Published by Allyn & Bacon, Boston, MA. © 2001 by Pearson Education. Reprinted by permission of the publisher.

Figure 2

THE COGNITIVE PROCESS DIMENSION

CATEGORIES & COGNITIVE PROCESSES	ALTERNATIVE NAMES	DEFINITIONS AND EXAMPLES
1. REMEMBER—Retrieve relevant knowledge from long-term memory		
1.1 RECOGNIZING	Identifying	Locating knowledge in long-term memory that is consistent with presented material (e.g., Recognize the dates of important events in history)
1.2 RECALLING	Retrieving	Retrieving relevant knowledge from long-term memory (e.g., Recall the dates of important events in history)
2. UNDERSTAND—Construct meaning from instructional messages, including oral, written, and graphic communication		
2.1 INTERPRETING	Clarifying, paraphrasing, representing, translating	Changing from one form of representation (e.g., numerical) to another (e.g., verbal—Paraphrase important speeches and documents)
2.2 EXEMPLIFYING	Illustrating, instantiating	Finding a specific example or illustration of a concept or principle (e.g., Give examples of various artistic painting styles)
2.3 CLASSIFYING	Categorizing, subsuming	Determining that something belongs to a category (e.g., a concept or principle—Classify observed or described cases of mental disorders)
2.4 SUMMARIZING	Abstracting, generalizing	Abstracting a general theme or major points (e.g., Write a short summary of the events portrayed on a videotape)
2.5 INFERRING	Concluding, extrapolating, interpolating, predicting	Drawing a logical conclusion from presented information (e.g., In learning a foreign language, infer grammatical principles from examples)
2.6 COMPARING	Contrasting, mapping, matching	Detecting correspondences between two ideas, objects, and the like (e.g., Compare historical events to contemporary situations)
2.7 EXPLAINING	Constructing models	Constructing a cause-effect model of a system (e.g., Explain the causes of important 18th-century events in France)

(Continued)

Figure 2 (Continued)

CATEGORIES & COGNITIVE PROCESSES	ALTERNATIVE NAMES	DEFINITIONS AND EXAMPLES
3.	**APPLY**—Carry out or use a procedure in a given situation	
3.1 EXECUTING	Carrying out	Applying a procedure to a familiar task (e.g., Divide one whole number by another whole number, both with multiple digits)
3.2 IMPLEMENTING	Using	Applying a procedure to an unfamiliar task (e.g., Use Newton's second law in situations in which it is appropriate)
4.	**ANALYZE**—Break material into its constituent parts and determine how the parts relate to one another in an overall structure	
4.1 DIFFERENTIATING	Discriminating, distinguishing, focusing, selecting	Distinguishing relevant from irrelevant parts or important from unimportant parts of presented material (e.g., Distinguish between relevant and irrelevant numbers in a mathematical word problem)
4.2 ORGANIZING	Finding coherence, integrating, outlining, parsing, structuring	Determining how elements fit or function with a structure (e.g., Structure evidence in a historical description into evidence for and against a particular historical explanation)
4.3 ATTRIBUTING	Deconstructing	Determining a point of view, bias, values, or intent underlying presented material (e.g., Determine the point of view of the author of an essay in terms of his or her political perspective)

CATEGORIES & COGNITIVE PROCESSES	ALTERNATIVE NAMES	DEFINITIONS AND EXAMPLES
5.	**EVALUATE**—Make judgments based on criteria and standards	
5.1 CHECKING	Coordinating, detecting, monitoring, testing	Detecting inconsistencies or fallacies within a process or product, determining whether a process or product has internal consistency, detecting the effectiveness of a procedure as it is being implemented (e.g., Determine if a scientist's conclusions follow from observed data)
5.2 CRITIQUING	Judging	Detecting inconsistencies between a product and external criteria, determining whether a product has external consistency, detecting the appropriateness of a procedure for a given problem (e.g., Judge which of two methods is the best way to solve a given problem)
6.	**CREATE**—Put elements together to form a coherent or functional whole; reorganize elements in a new pattern or structure	
6.1 GENERATING	Hypothesizing	Coming up with alternative hypotheses based on criteria (e.g., Generate hypotheses to account for an observed phenomenon)
6.2 PLANNING	Designing	Devising a procedure for accomplishing some task (e.g., Plan a research paper on a given historical topic)
6.3 PRODUCING	Constructing	Inventing a product (e.g., Build habitats for a specific purpose)

SOURCE: From Lorin W. Anderson and David R. Krathwohl, *A Taxonomy for Learning, Teaching, and Assessing: A Revision of Bloom's Taxonomy of Educational Objectives*. Published by Allyn & Bacon, Boston, MA. © 2001 by Pearson Education. Reprinted by permission of the publisher.

Resource G

*Sample School Districts
Using a Concept-Based Model
for Curriculum and Instruction*

1. Pomperaug Regional School District 15
   Middlebury, Connecticut
   Contact: Dr. Lois Lanning
   Assistant Superintendent
   llanning@region15.org

2. Laredo ISD
   Laredo, Texas
   Contact: Belinda Silva
   Advanced Academic Director
   bzsilva@laredoisd.org

3. Blue Valley School District #229
   Overland Park, Kansas
   Contacts: Charlotte McDonald
   Science Coordinating Teacher
   cmcdonald@bluevalleyk12.org
   Diane DeNoon
   Foreign Language Coordinating Teacher
   ddenoon@bluevalleyk12.org

4. Virginia Beach Public School
   Virginia Beach, Virginia
   Contact: Mary Ann Burritt
   Director of Gifted Education &
   Academy Programs
   MaryAnn.Burritt@VBSchools.com

5. Meridian School District
   Meridian, Idaho
   Contact: Dr. Linda Clark
   Superintendent
   clarkl@meridianschools.org

6. Round Rock ISD
   Round Rock, Texas
   Contact: Dr. Beverly Helfinstein
   Assistant Superintendent
   Beverly_Helfinstein@roundrockisd.org

7. Twin Valley Public Schools
   Elverson, Pennsylvania
   Contacts: Dr. Michael Leonard
   Assistant Superintendent
   mleonard@twinval.k12.pa.us
   Robert Pleis
   Director of Curriculum
   bpleis@twinal.k12.pa.us

8. Weston Public Schools
   Weston, Connecticut
   Contact: Richard Miller
   Assistant Superintendent
   Miller@westonk12-ct.org

9. Department of Defense Education Activity
   Arlington, Virginia
   Contact: Susan Karlesses
   Secondary English Language Arts Coordinator
   Susan.Karlesses@hq.dodea.edu

10. Tasmania, Australia
    Contact: Dr. Ruth Radford
    Tasmanian Government
    Assistant Director, Leadership and Learning
    School of Education Division
    ruth.radford@education.tas.gov.au

11. Cairo American College
    Cairo, Egypt
    Contact: Lillian Salama
    Teacher
    lsalama@cacegypt.org

References

Anderson, L. W., & Krathwohl, D. R. (Eds.). (2001). *A taxonomy for learning, teaching, and assessing: A revision of Bloom's taxonomy of educational objectives.* New York: Addison-Wesley Longman.

Bloom, B. S., Engelhart, M. D., Furst, E. J., Hill, W. H., & Krathwohl, D. R. (Eds.). (1956). *Taxonomy of educational objectives: The classification of educational goals: Handbook I. Cognitive domain.* New York: David McKay.

Bransford, J., Brown, A., & Cocking, R. (Eds.). (2000). *How people learn: Brain, mind, experience, and school* (Expanded ed.). Committee on Developments in the Science of Learning and Committee on Learning Research and Educational Practice, Commission on Behavioral and Social Sciences and Education, National Research Council. Washington, DC: National Academies Press.

Brooks, J. G., & Brooks, M. G. (1999). *In search of understanding: The case for constructivist classrooms* (Rev. ed.). Alexandria, VA: Association for Supervision and Curriculum Development.

Calvin, W. H. (1996). *How brains think.* New York: Basic Books.

Calvin, W. H., & Ojemann, G. A. (1994). *Conversations with Neil's brain: The neural nature of thought and language.* New York: Basic Books.

Center for American Progress/Institute for America's Future. (2005, August). *Getting smarter, becoming fairer: A progressive education agenda for a stronger nation.* Washington, DC: Author.

Cotton, K. (2003). *Principals and student achievement: What the research says.* Alexandria, VA: Association for Supervision and Curriculum Development.

Elmore, R. (2004). *School reform from the inside out: Policy, practice and performance.* Cambridge, MA: Harvard Educational Publishing Group.

Erickson, H. L. (1995). *Stirring the head, heart, and soul: Redefining curriculum and instruction.* Thousand Oaks, CA: Corwin Press.

Erickson, H. L. (2001). *Stirring the head, heart, and soul: Redefining curriculum and instruction* (2nd ed.). Thousand Oaks, CA: Corwin Press.

Erickson, H. L. (2002). *Concept-based curriculum and instruction: Teaching beyond the facts* (2nd ed.) Thousand Oaks, CA: Corwin Press.

Erickson, H. L. (2003). *Integrated curriculum: A chapter of the curriculum handbook.* Alexandria, VA: Association for Supervision and Curriculum Development.

Gardner, H. (1993). *Frames of mind: The theory of multiple intelligences.* New York: Basic Books.

Gardner, H. (1999). *The disciplined mind: What all students should understand.* New York: Simon & Schuster.

Mandler, J. M. (2004). *The foundations of mind.* New York: Oxford University Press.

National Intelligence Council. (2004). *Mapping the global future.* Washington, DC: Author.

Novak, J. D., & Gowin, B. (1999). *Learning how to learn.* Cambridge, UK: Cambridge University Press.

Paul, R. W. (1995a). *Making critical thinking intuitive.* Santa Rosa, CA: Foundation for Critical Thinking.

Paul, R. W. (1995b). *The logic of creative and critical thinking.* Santa Rosa, CA: Foundation for Critical Thinking.

Paul, R. W., & Elder, L. (2004a). *The thinker's guide to the nature and functions of critical and creative thinking.* Santa Rosa, CA: Foundation for Critical Thinking.

Paul, R. W., & Elder, L. (2004b). *The miniature guide to critical thinking concepts and tools.* Santa Rosa, CA: Foundation for Critical Thinking.

Pink, D. (2005). *A whole new mind: Moving from the information age to the conceptual age.* New York: Penguin Group, Riverhead Books.

Programme for International Student Assessment. (2003). *First results from PISA 2003, executive summary.* Washington, DC: Organization for Economic Co-operation and Development.

Ray, K. W. (1999). *Wondrous words: Writers and writing in the elementary classroom.* Urbana, IL: National Council of Teachers of English.

Ritchart, R. (2002). *Intellectual character: What it is, why it matters, and how to get it.* San Francisco: Jossey-Bass.

Robbins, P., & Alvey, H. (2004). *The new principal's fieldbook: Strategies for success.* Alexandria, VA: Association for Supervision and Curriculum Development.

Schlechty, P. C. (2005). *Creating great schools: Six critical systems at the heart of educational innovation.* San Francisco: Jossey-Bass.

Senge, P., Kleiner, A., Roberts, C., Ross, R., Roth, G., & Smith, B. (1999). *The dance of change: The challenges to sustaining momentum in learning organizations.* New York: Doubleday.

Sousa, D. A. (2001). *How the brain learns.* Thousand Oaks, CA: Corwin Press.

Sternberg, R. J. (Ed.). (2002). *Handbook of intelligence.* New York: Cambridge University Press.

Sylwester, R. (2003). *A biological brain in a cultural classroom* (2nd ed.). Thousand Oaks, CA: Corwin Press.

Sylwester, R. (2005). *How to explain a brain: An educator's handbook of brain terms and cognitive processes.* Thousand Oaks, CA: Corwin Press.

Taba, H. (1966). *Teaching strategies and cognitive functioning in elementary school children (cooperative research project)*. Washington, DC: Office of Education, U.S. Department of Health, Education, and Welfare.

Tomlinson, C. A., & Eidson, C. C. (2003a). *Differentiation in practice: A resource guide for differentiating curriculum, grades K–5*. Alexandria, VA: Association for Supervision and Curriculum Development.

Tomlinson, C. A., & Eidson, C. C. (2003b). *Differentiation in practice: A resource guide for differentiating curriculum, grades 5–9*. Alexandria, VA: Association for Supervision and Curriculum Development.

Tomlinson, C. A., & Strickland, C. A. (2005). *Differentiation in practice: A resource guide for differentiating curriculum, grades 9–12*. Alexandria, VA: Association for Supervision and Curriculum Development.

Wagner, T., Kegan, R., Laskow Lahey, L., Lemons, R., Garnier, J., Helsing, D., et al. (2005). *Change leadership: A practical guide to transforming schools*. San Francisco: Jossey-Bass.

Wiggins, G., & McTighe, J. (1999). *Understanding by design*. Alexandria, VA: Association for Supervision and Curriculum Development.

Wiggins, G., & McTighe, J. (2005). *Understanding by design* (Exp. 2nd ed.). Alexandria, VA: Association for Supervision and Curriculum Development.

Wolfe, P. (2001). *Brain matters: Translating research into classroom practice*. Alexandria, VA: Association for Supervision and Curriculum Development.

Index